Praise f

MW01230315

In these pages you will meet a couple of ranch intellectuals in overalls
who season their learning and their expansive curiosity with direct
observation and experience. Their minds already fed by Emerson,
Thoreau, the poets and novelists they've read, they continue to grow by
their engagement with the mountain world they live in. Two educators
who never stop learning, Clara and Margaret learn from one another,
they learn from the Appaloosas they raise; they learn from the deer
on the ridge and the elk over the far hill. They learn from the frequent
strays, the students or the lost who come to stay for a time and go back
into the world healed or healing, and brave enough to find their own way.
Never rich or famous these women enrich the lives of all who make their
way to Singing Acres Ranch. If you haven't been there yet, their friend,
author Carol Ann Wilson, will show you the way. From the three of them
you will learn something of the height, depth, and breadth our human
spirits can reach.

GARY HOLTHAUS
Author of *Wide Skies: Finding a Home in the West* and *From the Farm to the
Table: What All Americans Need to Know about Agriculture*

Here is a book about two ostensibly ordinary women—Clara Reida
and Margaret Locarnini—whose lives instead have what's necessary
to become legend—dreams, adventure, risk, determination, humor,
generosity, struggle, compassion, triumph, and loss. Carol Wilson has
captured the spirited lives of these two life-long friends through layered
stories—Clara's and Margaret's—as well as those of friends, students,
neighbors, family members, and sometimes strangers. One cannot help
but feel the vibrant resonance that emanates from these two visionaries
and the singular place called Singing Acres Ranch.

CAROLYN SERVID
Author of *Of Landscape and Longing: Finding a Home at the Water's Edge*

Because We Wanted To!

Other titles by
Carol Ann Wilson:

*Still Point of the Turning World:
The Life of Gia-fu Feng*

About Earline

Because We Wanted To!

Two women, a dream,
and a ranch called
Singing Acres

Carol Ann Wilson

BOULDER, COLORADO

ISBN: 978-1517151614 (print)

www.carolannwilson.info
E-book available

Editing: Laura Goodman
Cover and text design: Sue Campbell
Cover photos: "Margaret and Clara" courtesy, *The Sunday Chieftain*;
"RJ" (horse) courtesy, B. Casapulla, Singing Acres view by Carol Wilson

Dedication image: Frank Mechau, *Five Horses*, 1930
Crayon and pencil on paper, 14 x 18 1/8 inches
Friends of the Fine Arts Center Purchase Fund, FA1949.8
Collection of the Colorado Springs Fine Arts Center

Printed in the United States of America

To honor and remember our Margarets
Margaret Ann Locarnini &
Margaret Susan Wilson

Contents

INTRODUCTION

THE SILVER-WHITE SANGRE DE CRISTO PEAKS DAZZLED, BURSTING IN sight as I rounded a tight curve on Colorado Highway 96, dropping down into the Wet Mountain Valley en route to the picturesque town of Westcliffe. I'd passed Singing Acres Ranch a few minutes earlier, seen the smoke rising in the crisp early morning air from the wood stove chimney in the one hundred-plus year-old ranch house, and knew Clara and Margaret would be well past their morning chores. My heart tugged, but I hadn't stopped because the auction would start soon, the auction that my sister was staking everything she had on. And she didn't know I was coming. Having driven the hundred and fifty miles from Denver, I now needed to find her before the day's events began to unfold, or unravel.

Our big-sister, little-sister relationship sometimes got tangled in assumptions based on our respective temperaments, which differed considerably. Those differences weren't a simple dichotomy such as extrovert, introvert, or analytical versus impetuous. Susan viewed me as more conventional and possibly predictable, whereas Susan came to her own conclusions based on considerations I didn't always know existed and didn't always understand. We both were trying to find our way in the world; we both strove for independence and self-sufficiency, and we shared a struggle to mend from dysfunction in the family as a whole.

My little sister, Susan, my only sister, and I were connected at the heart, but even then in our forties, we found at times we had to tread carefully with each other. I felt unsure about intruding on her monumental day. Funny, I know, that I was unsure about what to do when it came to the person I loved most in the world, but I was. Looking back, even I find this hard to believe.

But at that time, since I couldn't rely on my own judgment, I turned to the person whose judgment I trusted most—Clara. Solid, down to earth, salt of the earth, some would say, Clara seemed to sense and understand things deeply. Maybe this was because she worked with and knew horses and kids, or because she paid close attention to whomever she was with and whatever she did, or maybe all of this plus something more. The attention she paid was always that deep kind, as if she were absorbing everything a person said, along with their very presence. Another big factor was that she knew Susan, and she knew me.

I felt safe with Clara and I knew that she would either give me good advice or say she didn't have any to give. On two critical sisterly occasions, she did guide me, and for both occasions I would always be grateful. The auction was the first. Unable to let the event just slide by, I'd phoned Clara the night before.

"I can't reach Susan and I don't want to be the overbearing older sister and intrude. But I also want to be there, just to support her. What do you think? Should I go?"

Without a pause she said, "Oh, yes. You should go."

And there I was. Driving through the almost deserted streets, looking for the Dodge pickup Susan had been using lately, I thought I recognized it in front of the little hometown café. When I didn't find her in the café, I asked for directions to the courthouse.

She was standing on the courthouse lawn with several other people, some she'd known through the community at Stillpoint, the land she was trying to save. She'd been left a share of that land, and the other two owners had sold their shares to a local lawyer who'd sold it to developers. The developers' trying to force Susan to sell her share and her determination to save the land from development took the dispute to court. The judge had ruled in favor of a public auction of the land and here we were, each of us gearing up for it.

She saw me walking across the courthouse lawn, and I saw her face light up. Framed by her long, dark hair, her blue eyes were shining, and a broad smile graced her lips. Clara had been right. That realization marked a precious moment in a significant day.

To raise the necessary funds, she and I had secured a bank loan for about sixty percent of what we anticipated paying, and several friends were putting up the rest. Mary, one of those friends, along with Carmen who had introduced Susan to her, was in the group.

The sheriff soon appeared and signaled the auction was about to start. Susan and I both were novices at auctions, and there were several times we collectively held our breath as the bidding went higher and higher between the developers and us. Then, as Susan made another bid, we watched the two developers consult with their attorney. They wouldn't go higher. We'd succeeded in outbidding them. We'd bought Stillpoint, all one hundred sixty-six acres of its meadows and forest.

ONLY A FEW WEEKS LATER, IN APRIL OF 1991, I AGAIN TURNED TO CLARA. Susan had left several messages on my answering machine to say the stomach problems she'd been having recently had landed her in the Gillette, Wyoming hospital.

"Hey, Little Sister," for she liked to reverse the roles, and there were many times when that was completely appropriate, when the five years between us reordered themselves. Younger Susan's wisdom belied birth order. And she liked to remind me that I was an inch shorter. "Guess I'll be in the hospital for some tests. I'll try to call again, but I'm not sure when I can."

She'd been staying in Gillette with friend and companion, Mickey DeWeese, a childhood friend of Clara's. The local doctor she'd seen wanted to do some intensive tests, which would take a few days. Again, I tried but couldn't reach my sister. No answer at home, no phone in her hospital room. I called Clara.

"I think I should go. Do you think it's okay? Will she think I'm interfering?"

"Well, it doesn't matter if she does think that, but I doubt she will. You should go." Dear, dear Clara.

The earliest flight I could take landed me in Gillette midday. Mickey picked me up at the airport and we went straight to the hospital. There was Susan, sitting up in the bed, hospital gown enveloping her slight body, her long hair draped over her shoulder, a stack of files beside her as she wrote furiously on a legal pad. She was a lawyer, after all, and she had work to do.

The tests began the next morning. Within a day or two the doctor determined she had a benign tumor in her stomach, and that surgery would take care of it. But that's not what happened. What happened was that the tumor was malignant, and it had metastasized. Then the doctor thought maybe she would have a year.

I was stunned and terrified. Later when Susan came out of the anesthesia and I told her about the cancer, she was surprised, but more accepting than I. She said something that I hadn't known, something that reflected that mysterious "otherness" that set her apart. "I've been told several times that I wouldn't have a very long life. But I thought I would make it to forty-six." She was forty-one.

There were complications from the surgery. Susan weighed about ninety pounds before the operation. Her body was frail and the surgery weakened her further. She had to undergo more surgery, and her body just couldn't take it. She died ten days after the initial operation.

I wasn't there. Thinking she would have more time, she and I agreed I should keep the commitment to be part of a teacher-education review team in Idaho. It would help pay the first installment on our loan for Stillpoint, and I would be gone only a week. Then I'd be back with her and we would figure out what our next steps would be. Our brother, Bruce, who lived in Alaska, and our mother, who lived in the Florida panhandle, arrived in the meantime.

Bruce, the eldest of us three, proved a profound source of strength and caring. He stayed with Susan, watched after our mother, and kept me up to date on how things were. When they started to go downhill fast, he called to let me know right away. When the distance and complications of travel from Moscow, Idaho to Gillette, Wyoming prevented me from getting to Susan before she died, he was a source of solace.

I didn't get to be with Susan when she died, but I did get to be with her as the preceding events unfolded, thanks to that nudge and confirmation from Clara. I'll always have those precious times to hold close. And when we gathered on the sunny hillside at Stillpoint to commemorate Susan's life and spread her ashes as she'd wished, Clara asked to spread them.

There under that startlingly blue sky, in the warm May afternoon, the unusual gathering of ranchers, tribal representatives, lawyers, educators, and contemplatives watched and attended as Clara dipped her hand in the simple square wooden box, then held it high and open for the breeze to carry the precious dust across the accepting meadow.

DO YOU KNOW WHAT IT'S LIKE WHEN YOU CAN'T EVEN REMEMBER MEETing someone dear to you because it seems impossible that he or she hasn't always been a part of your life? That's how I feel about Clara and Margaret. How could it be that I didn't know them before 1988 when Susan introduced us? I felt that warm connection right off the bat, so that may be why I feel this way. Or maybe the friendship is so embedded in my life because after Susan was gone, I still had them, and they provided a reflection of an important part of her life, even though it was only three years of it. But it was the last three years. Susan had connected us, and it was a connection that was to continually strengthen, not break. Susan was part of that. Even after Margaret died in 2007, sixteen years after Susan, the friendship of the four of us lived on in that of Clara's and mine. It built on a loving foundation, and it grew. It grows now.

In 2009, two years after Margaret died, I completed and published a book about the life of Gia-fu Feng. His partial autobiography, three-hundred pages of stream-of-consciousness writings primarily about his early life in China that Susan and Clara had been editing in those months before Susan's death, formed the foundation. Susan's connection to and care of Stillpoint framed Gia-fu's story. Many interviews, much research, rewriting and rewriting produced a book. Clara read it and liked it, which made me very happy. Not only was she was a critic of Gia-fu's, but she had been a highly successful and demanding English teacher. I felt I'd passed a tough class.

She told me how much she'd enjoyed the book, then she went on to say, "People keep asking me when I'll write about what Margaret and I have done. I've saved newspaper clippings and other artifacts thinking someday I might do that. Now it seems like an awful lot of work for someone who's trying to do less work. But I know someone who *could* do it." I'm sure my jaw dropped when she leveled her steady gaze at me.

"I'd love to write about you and Margaret," I managed to say, feeling nothing but highly honored at the suggestion, though already feeling the anxiety about whether I could do it justice.

For Clara, this brief conversation proved another case of not knowing what she was getting into, just as she and Margaret didn't know what would come of their initial meeting with my sister or with each other, for that matter.

Clara probably had a few stories in mind. For my part, I figured I had an opportunity to really explore the lives of two amazing women who led distinctive lives, who did so much for others—and Clara continues to do—who were courageous, delightful and just ornery enough for me to want to dig into the archeology of their lives. And most of all, who were so important to my sister, and who became as sisters to Susan, and then to me.

A layer of that archeology has to do with independence. Independence and self-sufficiency ranked high in this country's early values. It fueled the pioneering spirit of earlier centuries, and it lived and lives on, thankfully, in people like Margaret, Clara, and Susan. These women didn't react against accepted roles for women. They simply found them irrelevant, moving forward with their own dreams, and to their respective degrees, realizing those dreams. That's independence.

Easy as it is to accept someone as ready-made, to think this is how they are and this is how they've always been, it's far more intriguing and astonishing to have the opportunity to discover what has gone into shaping someone's life, to ponder the artifacts, features and cultural landscapes that have affected heart and soul. In doing so, you realize that our relationship with another is only a small part of the other's life, whether friend, sister or mother. And then questions arise, previously unimagined, and following those questions leads to more and often deeper questions.

My hope in finding and following the questions, in exploring and writing about these two lives, the history of Clara and Margaret, is certainly to share a story of adventure, courage, and inspiration. It's also to gain insight into how the whole of their experience brought them to be who they came to be and how they affected so many lives. Perhaps though, first and foremost I seek a way to honor friendship, the kind that Clara and Margaret had, that nourished Susan, and that Clara and I still delight in. The kind that has affected so many people whose lives these women touched. In doing so, I hope to acknowledge and pay tribute to a larger circle of friendship that ripples outward without end.

PART I
The Trail to Singing Acres Ranch

Clara, wearing her first pair of real cowboy boots, on Queen, circa 1951.
Courtesy Clara.

1

Girl Scouts on Horseback

I'VE HEARD IT SAID THAT THE SLIGHTEST THING CAN SOMETIMES change the direction of our lives. Although in retrospect not slight at all, Clara and Margaret's meeting at the Flying G Ranch did just that, it set them on a single path the two had only previously dreamed of.

Some might call their encounter a matter of fate, destiny, or providence. I call it luck. In this case, it was luck the two of them wouldn't realize for a whole year. Despite the delay, their friendship did begin, and when it did, it created a trajectory all its own.

I was curious about how it all happened, assuming from the time I'd first met them they'd been friends right off the bat. It was hard to imagine otherwise because their friendship was so solid those thirty-some years later. A good example of accepting something as ready-made, I thought, without understanding what had transpired to create it. A worthy lesson for me, and a good opportunity to dig into what had shaped these two lives and their friendship.

Through numerous talks with Clara, her friends and family, images of those years began to take form in my mind. Knowing how time can blur memories, how events can conflate, a picture developed nonetheless, likely along with a few inaccuracies in sequence and timing.

Clara was at the Flying G the summer before Margaret arrived, and the next year, Clara's second, Margaret's first, the two met. But it was the third summer that provided an opportunity for a friendship to begin. And then everything changed. But let's start in the middle with their meeting, or how I imagine it, then fill in the rest.

1957

HIGH IN THE ROCKY MOUNTAINS, OUT FROM DECKERS, COLORADO, Girl Scout camp was gearing up at the Flying G Ranch. Clara, having completed her junior year at Kansas State Teachers College of Pittsburg, was back for the second year as camp counselor and member of the riding staff. Her first year was memorable, a doozy in many ways, but it was so good she wanted to come back.

Walking to the corral that first morning, she breathed in the crisp air, pungent with high mountain fir, pine and aspen. She felt invigorated, ready for anything. She gazed at that deep azure blue sky you see only in the high country, watched a few puffs of cotton-ball clouds floating lazily in it, and thought again how much she loved this country. She wanted to stay here forever.

She felt eager to be back to work with the horses and the kids, too, even if all of her friends from last year hadn't returned. With these thoughts running through her mind, Clara gathered her horse's gear and began to saddle up. In the process, she spied a young woman about her age whom she didn't recognize standing beside a horse, saddle in hand. The newcomer was watching Clara's every move. Clara saw Newcomer hesitate a moment, then plop the saddle on her horse's back, centering it about right. But then Newcomer stepped back and looked at the cinch as if it had just floated down from Mars.

Walking over to the short, slender woman, Clara noticed she was about her own height, give or take an inch. "Clara Reida," she said, wanting to be friendly. She was remembering her own first summer there. "Rago, Kansas."

"Margaret Locarnini. Oakland, California," the other said, reaching out a hand to shake Clara's. Clara noticed her grip was firm and strong, just like her voice.

"Oakland. That's pretty far away. What brings you here?" Although she knew counselors came from all over, she hadn't yet met one from California. Several of her closest friends here were from Colorado. A few from Kansas.

"I've been a Girl Scout for a long time. Started with the Daisies in first grade and stayed with it. I was looking for a summer job away from home, and my friend Mac thought I oughta try this. It'll help pay next year's tuition for my teaching degree."

Clara noted Margaret's steady gaze as she returned the question, "How about you?"

"Kind of like you," Clara said, thinking about just how similar their situations were. She told Margaret about her need to pay college tuition, since she was studying to be a teacher, too. And she told her about being here last year and loving it.

She didn't want to offend this new acquaintance, but she thought she could use some help, so she asked, "Have you done this much?"

She registered Margaret's sly grin and noticed that her eyes held both relief and wariness as she admitted, "Not much. But if you show me once, you won't have to show me again."

Walking around to the other side of the horse, Clara pulled the cinch and stirrup down before she went back to the left. She knew she was doing these things automatically, but she wanted to be thorough and careful for this eager learner. She hooked the left stirrup over the saddle horn, reached under the horse, pulled and threaded the cinch through the rings, wondering just how many times she had done this. Quite a few. But from the way Margaret watched and followed, Clara knew that what she'd said was true. She wouldn't have to show her again.

And that was that. Clara and Margaret didn't see each other much afterwards. Clara still had wrangling and horse management on her list and Margaret was just learning the ropes in terms of horses, spending much of her time working with the kids.

That's the middle of the Flying G story, this meeting, this slight thing that became a crucial one. Now to return to the beginning to find out what Clara's first summer had brought, and then some of her second, before returning to the one that changed their lives.

1956

CLARA HEARD ABOUT THE GIRL SCOUT CAMP FROM LOLLY, A GOOD friend in Pratt. Having just graduated from Pratt Junior College and going on to Kansas State Teachers College in the fall, Clara was talking with her friend about needing to find a job to pay for that next year. That's when Lolly told her she should go work for the Girl Scouts at one of their ranches outside Denver. "You love horses, you're studying to be a teacher, and you can teach kids to ride."

She'd done what Lolly suggested—sent off for the application, filled it out as soon as she got it, shot it back, and then got hired, it seemed like on the spot. It seemed the Girl Scout Council, despite her never having been a Girl Scout, had liked that she had so much experience with horses, and that was what had added wrangling to her list of duties. Later she realized that somehow she'd gotten a reputation before she'd even set foot on the ranch. And, she'd come to understand, that horse reputation meant she'd get assigned the green critters. As for working with the girls, her involvement in saddle club and lots of other activities, and, of course, that she was studying to be a teacher must have caught their attention, too. Good references had probably iced the cake.

The job would pay well enough for her to cover most of her college expenses for next year. She'd been excited to be hired and had accepted right away. But then the first few days as she rode up and down those steep slopes, she wondered why she'd been so excited. She was a flat-lander, not at all accustomed to mountains, the seemingly perpendicular ground, loose rock, and all the holes, some of them partially hidden under grasses or scrubby bushes. The terrain at all angles, rock, dirt, holes. She felt bug-eyed.

Yet, she had a lot of faith in horses and knew they knew what they were doing. So she just hung on figuring that at some point, she really would get the hang of it.

Back at the barn in the days after those early rides, Clara watched to make sure the girls did things properly. She'd already been working with them on taking care of the horses and now she looked to see that they were checking for saddle sores or scratches on their legs and picking out their feet for pebbles or anything else that could cause bruising. She was happy with what she saw; these girls were learning.

Pleased that the program covered horse care and stable responsibilities, along with horsemanship and trail riding, Clara knew these kids were learning more than just getting on a horse and galloping off. That part they did love, sure, but they seemed to appreciate what went along with it, too. She felt she was pretty good at teaching them the whole range of skills and duties and they trusted her and would try things they may not otherwise have wanted to.

As for her own learning, Slim was a big help in getting her acclimated. When he'd first seen her riding, he'd hollered, using her camp name, "Bird, for God's sake, get your heels down!"

How was she to know? She hadn't grown up on saddles. She grew up riding bareback. Her dad hadn't let the kids ride a saddle, and after he died, her mom wouldn't either. She didn't get to have one until she started riding with the Saddle Club with the neighbor lady, and that hadn't been all that long ago. It could've been hard to overcome a habit that was so ingrained. But Slim's admonition made that habit history. Her heels were down.

Slim himself was a true cowhand, and Clara looked up to him. Tall and wiry-thin, he sure looked the part. He'd taken care of the last of the United States Army mounts, and cared for the polo horses at the Broadmoor resort in Colorado Springs, working a lot of different matches there. With all his vast experience, Clara knew she could learn a great deal from him.

For his part, Slim knew Clara had considerable riding experience and thought she was a good rider. She soon had a chance to hear it directly from him. "Obviously, you can ride, so I want you to be down here at the barn in the morning at 5:00. There's a locoed horse we have to get off the mountain."

Clara didn't know much about locoed horses, but she soon learned. Horses addicted to locoweed, a sweet plant that tastes kind of like alfalfa, act unpredictably, especially when they get warmed up. You won't have any idea there's anything wrong, then the horse can start to sweat, shy at bushes, have kicking fits, and generally just act nuts. Slim hoped to cure this horse. He'd never had an opportunity to try it, and he was set on doing so. With a philosophy that any malady you needed to doctor a horse for was in your kitchen cabinet, he'd had quite a successful record. He had his heart set on putting it to use again it in this case.

At 5:00 the next morning, they went after the horse. Slim had spotted the little mare the day before. It was a good ride from the ranch, but they found her, standing in a meadow, cut to ribbons from walking through fences and all kinds of brush, unaware of any obstacles in her search for locoweed. Slim instructed Clara, "I'm going to get ahead of her, and you're going to get behind her. Don't try to lead her, she won't lead, But if you can get her following my horse and you keep encouraging her from behind, maybe we can get her down to the barn."

After a half-day of careful maneuvering, they finally got the poor animal into Slim's corral. And for the next month Clara knew Slim was working steadily with her, watched him attending the wounds armed with his old orange medicine box full of kitchen magic. To the deeper effects of locoweed he applied patient attention. Then one day the horse disappeared, just like that. When Clara saw the empty corral and looked at Slim, the question clear in her eyes, he shrugged and said, "You can't cure 'em."

She'd been so hopeful in light of Slim's skill and care. She knew miracles were in rare supply, but still, she'd been so hopeful. Now she had to accept there was no hope for that horse. It was so sad.

Clara had met Kas, the riding director, whose name was Virginia Kasdorf, before camp began. Knowing Clara would be new to the riding staff, Kas had invited her to come to Denver and ride down to camp with her. Clara's mom drove her to Denver, and the two young women went from there. Their interest in horses a natural link, they developed a liking and respect for each other right off the bat.

One day she and Kas were looking over some new horses that had been brought in. Clara watched Kas lock her eyes on a pretty little black and white Welsh-pony looking horse, short, just like Kas. The little thing was acting pretty spirited, throwing its head, stamping, not still for a second. She suspected Kas was gobsmacked, a fact Kas confirmed right away. "*That's* gonna be my horse."

Before Clara knew what was happening, Kas grabbed the horse's reins and started to get on. She saw the horse explode, jumping so hard that the force threw Kas completely off, despite her considerable riding experience, dumping her in the dirt. Although Clara didn't like to butt into someone else's business, she felt herself reacting automatically as she grabbed the reins and swung up into the saddle. She knew to keep the horse's head up, and she knew how to do it. She was getting quite a ride as the horse leapt and lunged around the corral, but she knew it couldn't buck all that hard with its head in that position.

She'd learned early on, as a little kid, when she'd climb up on a stump and get on a horse bareback, to keep their heads up and just hang on. Riding them was what broke them. She didn't know there was any other way to do it. Didn't know about running them around in circles with lunge lines and all that. It worked for her, and she turned out a lot of safe horses. And the reason was that she would be with a horse and couldn't stand it if she couldn't ride it. So she broke it the only way she knew how. True, she got flung around quite a bit, but she broke those horses.

Now, finally Clara felt the little horse wear down. She rode over to where Kas was leaning on the corral rail. "I don't think she's so bad, really." She slapped a fly from the horse's shoulder. "I think we can get her out of this."

"Well, you'd better be the one to ride her," Kas snapped.

Clara did ride her. Patchy was her personal horse for several weeks, and she had a ball on her. She figured little Patchy had probably just been spoiled. She'd probably tossed somebody off and they never touched her again. Maybe she'd been given to a kid who couldn't manage her. She believed the horse just hadn't been thoroughly trained.

After a few weeks, Clara realized Patchy was ready and reliable, would even let someone as wary as Kasdorf on her, a good sign all around. But she'd grown attached to the horse. Nevertheless, hard as it was to give her up, she knew Patchy would be great for the girls and that they would love her. It did her proud, for both the horse and the girls, that they did.

There were many facets of being in the mountains an inexperienced flatlander had to get used to, not just the varying terrain. One night with supper eaten and evening chores done, in the mountain darkness Clara started the hike back to her unit and her tent. At least she didn't have night duty, something that didn't happen often. She didn't mind it at all, but she also didn't mind a break. Following the little path, she made her way along, thinking how good bed was going to feel.

The ranch seemed big and sprawling, especially at night, and she guessed with more than three hundred acres, it was. Plenty of room for the older and younger age camps with their various units. No moon tonight, but with millions of stars overhead and flashlight in hand she hiked on.

She heard a noise, something rustling through the bushes. Images of bears flitted through her mind, and her heart ramped up a few beats. She didn't know what was making the noise, and she didn't know what to do. Crouching down behind a bush, she heard it coming closer, closer. The dark felt like a black cloth draped over her. She could hardly breathe. Closer, closer. The flashlight her only available weapon, she thought if she shone the light in the thing's eyes, it would blind it and she could get away. Closer still. Now! She pointed the flashlight in the direction of the noise and pushed the switch. There it was. Looking down a long face right into her face were big, brown mournful eyes. A burro.

Clara sighed deeply. Several times. Feeling nothing but elation in seeing that long-eared, docile animal, Clara turned her face upward and told the stars. "At least it's equine, and that I can deal with."

Reaching her tent unmolested by bear or burro, Clara thanked her lucky stars again and, entering it, was happy to see only a human, and one who was ready to crawl into bed. Her tent-mate Dorothy Jo was bright, solid, and all-around wonderful. Clara got a kick out of her camp name, Pfadi, which she thought could be a rough translation from Norwegian for trailmaker. Dorothy Jo certainly was that.

When they met, Clara knew they liked each other instantly, and she had a feeling this friendship wouldn't be just a passing camp acquaintance. Remarkable that Pfadi was a premed student and that she'd gotten so lucky to have her as her own tent mate. Pfadi had already helped her adjust to the camp, had helped keep her grounded through all these new experiences. No matter what the hour, she was there to talk things over.

"Geez, what happened to you? You look like you saw a ghost!" The look on Pfadi's face matched the concern in her voice.

Clara told her about the burro, and soon they both were gasping with laughter. Yep, Pfadi helped her keep her feet on the ground.

She realized how much she enjoyed working with horses and kids and wanted that to be part of her life going forward—and it would be. She loved the laughter and fun with her friends, particularly when creativity was called for. She and some pals formed a jug and bottle band, and she marveled at all the talent they had there right under their noses. Monk, the camp name for Jeanene Jackson, on the piano and singing, and Lolly on the tub drum. Lolly knew Spanish songs from her time in Peru on a Fulbright.

Clara herself got a kick out of writing songs—parodies of popular hits or Gilbert and Sullivan that she and her friends could perform. Taking every opportunity, even quiet time in the saddle, when she was bringing up the tail on a trail ride, she'd come up with lyrics, plays, melodramas. Riding and writing, balancing a pad on the big silver-decorated horn of her old black saddle. She couldn't do that when she was in the lead, but the easy pace and quiet surroundings when riding tail seemed to stir her creative process, and she couldn't let the chance get by.

Music had always been important to her, starting with her family, who were all musical. And, there had been literary evenings back in

Adams, Kansas at which she'd been asked to perform. Once a month she'd find herself before an audience singing away. Then she'd been offered a scholarship at Friends University in Wichita and would've been traveling worldwide with the choir. After lots of deliberation, though, she opted for a much smaller scholarship at the junior college because she rated her confidence in her academic preparation for college pretty low. That choice had turned out well for academic reasons, and she'd also had plenty of jobs from sororities, fraternities, and all kinds of organizations singing, emceeing talent shows, doing stand-up comedy to help her with expenses. Now she was putting that talent and experience to work here. She loved it.

When their camp invited the other camp, Tomahawk, over for an evening's entertainment, they put on quite a show. Dorothy Jo and her floppy hat were kind of an emblem for the unit, and her nickname Pfadi made it that much better. So with a tip of the cowgirl hat to Gilbert and Sullivan, Clara saw her own *The Fanciful Flight of Fat Pfad Finderella* on stage.

It was great fun, and Clara couldn't get enough of the merriment her lyrics caused. She prized one part the girls kept repeating, all of them erupting in laughter every time they sang:

> "Camp counselor, Camp Counselor, there is in my unit
> a big, big, big, big, black horse!"
> "Does he have a halter on?"
> "No! He's naaa-ked!"

Not only did everyone laugh and clap, but she soon came to see the moral of the story hit home with the kids, again confirming her theory that learning and having fun go hand in hand. The girls had taken to heart that putting your elbows on the table resulted in killing a fairy. Finderella would go tell all the other fairies and they'd cry. Crying made rain, and rain kept you from horseback riding. It was becoming part of the camp lore, and Clara often saw the girls reminding each other of the consequences if their elbows happened to rest on the table. "You're making it rain!"

Clara liked that her light-hearted writing efforts had such good results. And it wasn't just those. The next summer, word would come to her that the progression program for Girl Scout western horseback riding badges that she'd worked on while grounded after a horse accident might be adopted nationally. She would be thrilled then, too.

As the summer went on, Clara realized the joy in being in such beauty and the camaraderie with the other counselors more than helped balance out the energy that went into dealing with difficult horses and tricky terrain. She knew she just needed more experience with both, and she was determined to stick around to get it. She'd fallen in love with the country. These mountains were magnificent, the air clean, crisp, and fragrant with pine, spruce and fir. The sky a blue she couldn't have imagined before, and the stars so brilliant and numerous they boggled the mind.

Fun, friends and some trials, too. Clara was feeling more comfortable riding on that steep, up and down terrain, so when the call came for a rescue team in the wee hours one morning, she was glad to be part of it. Learning that the mission entailed a long ride then a rescue down a rockslide where a Girl Scout had been injured when pushed down it by a burro, she recognized the challenges and accepted them.

She met up with the rest of the rescue team at the barn. The high-altitude air felt chilly on her face, more noticeable from having just crawled out of her warm bed. She noted those faithful stars twinkling and watching from above. Listening closely as Slim, who knew the country and the horses, advised them about which horses to take, Clara felt bolstered by his competent presence. "Take the horses with the littlest feet. They'll be better on tricky ground, and especially on that rockslide."

Saddled up and on their way by 2:00 a.m., Clara knew they were facing a five-hour ride each way, plus the time to rescue the girl and get her to safety. It would be a long haul, with all kinds of terrain to cover and a rockslide to negotiate. A challenge, but there was a kid who needed help, and that made any concerns melt away.

Reaching the rockslide along with the others, Clara dismounted and led her horse onto it. Badger dutifully picked his way across taking slow precise steps. She allowed him to move at his own careful pace as they traveled across and down to reach the hurt scout.

Relief came as they examined the girl and determined she wasn't hurt as badly as they'd feared. Still, the kid had taken quite a fall and Clara's first-aid training and experience with accidents told her they couldn't be completely sure of the extent of her injuries until a professional examined her fully. She could tell the girl was trying to be brave and the fall had really scared her.

Clara helped wrap soft pads around her and lift her onto the particularly gentle horse they'd brought. Then they worked their way back across the rockslide. At one point they had to take the girl off the horse, then remount her at a more stable spot. It all now felt like familiar, though treacherous, territory to Clara, and she was glad when they reached the trail where a pickup truck met them to take the girl to be examined and treated.

Their mission accomplished, Clara breathed out a huge sigh, making her wonder if she'd been breathing at all for a while. They'd accomplished what they'd set out to do, the girl was safe, and she'd negotiated more difficult terrain. Now she could relax, and she reminded herself to keep breathing.

Riding along at an easy pace so as not to further drain the weary horses, she felt her head slump forward, tug at the back of her neck, and her head jolt back up. She was so tired. So sleepy. Nodding off again and again during the interminable ride back to camp, she whispered her thanks to the good Badger for knowing his way home. But she thought it kind of amazing that she didn't just slide right out of the saddle during one of those little naps. Mainly she wondered how anything could be so thrilling as that mission. She didn't want anyone else to get hurt, but if someone did, she'd be the first to sign up to help, mountain terrain be damned.

1957

Back for the second year, Clara realized her reputation for working with horses continued to bring her tough ones to deal with. And although she felt good about her ability to work with those animals, she knew she couldn't let herself feel overly confident. Confident, sure, but not overly so. She also understood that she couldn't let down her guard, especially since she seemed to get the most difficult horses. And some of them were downright nasty.

She put Cisco in the nasty category. Eight new horses in the string this summer, and Cisco was one of them. Keeping herself on alert, Clara noticed everyone clamoring to ride the handsome white one. His being small didn't fool her. She thought he was a dangerous little booger. She couldn't figure out why the riding director, who unfortunately wasn't Kasdorf this year, wanted to keep him, even after Clara had ridden him quite a bit and he'd still tossed a few people.

Concerned with the girls' safety, she told the director, "Okay. If we're keeping Cisco, I'm riding him and only me. I know he's gonna charge a line one of these times and somebody's gonna get hurt. A kid can't hold him."

Clara thought the boss must have finally seen the problem because she agreed. For the next two days, Clara was committed to riding Cisco constantly, over all kinds of ground, thinking to work him as much as she possibly could. Toward the end of the second day, after Clara had hung on through three bucking rampages during a one-hour ride, she'd had it. She knew he wasn't fit for kids or even being around kids.

Clara knew she didn't get angry often or easily, but this situation was making her hot, and she let the camp director know just how hot. "I know I'm not in charge here, but if that horse is still here tomorrow, I'm outa here. He's not safe. He's not safe for me, he's not safe for anybody, and I can't make him safe. He's not trainable anymore. He's beyond it."

Clara couldn't interpret the look she got back. She thought it was a funny one and didn't know what lay behind it. When the woman didn't respond to Clara's words, Clara turned on her heel and left, not knowing what would happen.

The next morning when she went to work new horses, she didn't see Cisco anywhere. She knew he was gone. The director never said a word to her about it.

Working with about a hundred kids whose ages ranged from nine to sixteen could've been tough, but these young girls were great, with just enough orneriness to be healthy and make things more interesting. About the worst thing she'd seen any of them do was occasionally hold a horse back so they'd have to trot to catch up. They really liked to trot. But Clara knew what a bad thing this could be in a line, since everybody could be affected by what one person did, especially if it was sudden or out of the ordinary. Luckily, the girls listened to her and had learned that if they rode the way they were supposed to, they'd have plenty of opportunity to go faster.

Going fast or slow, even on level ground, she knew accidents could happen, especially with horses that hadn't learned all their lessons, that hadn't been worked out of bad habits. She put Chester, a beautiful buckskin gelding, in the category of "horses with bad habits." Because of his inclination to take the bit in his teeth when he wanted to go where he wanted to go, he could be trouble, although she was working with him on that. She liked him a lot, but she knew she couldn't let the girls ride him yet.

She was thinking about the girls and their progress as she was rounding up and bringing in the horses. She was riding Chester, and they were heading toward the corral. Next thing she knew, he'd taken the bit and pulled them toward a point in the fence. She felt his sudden movement and their closeness to the fence and then her hand hit the top of the post. A stab of pain shot through it as she felt it split apart. Almost in the same instant she sensed something happening to her kneecap. She heard a crack and pain seared through it. God, that hurt, it was awful. But the hurt didn't begin to match her anger. She was hot. She felt it rush all through her, and she knew the moment for learning was now.

Gritting her teeth, she turned her full attention to the horse, reining him this way and that, again and again, making him work as hard as she thought he'd ever worked. Only when she knew he had learned his lesson, when he obeyed her every command instantly, did she stop. Then she felt certain Chester wouldn't be pulling that bit business again.

She turned her attention to herself about the same time help arrived. She saw Sunny rushing over to her with the medic. Apparently, she'd seen the accident and had run for help. Clara was relieved it'd come right away.

At the clinic, she learned her hand needed stitches, and her kneecap was fractured. The doctor told her the hand would heal pretty quickly, but the fractured kneecap would have to be in a cast for about three weeks. No horseback riding for her at all. Grounded. She couldn't believe it. No riding. Would she lose her job? Get shipped back to Kansas? Miss the chance to be here at the Flying G the rest of the summer?

She lay on the bed pondering the situation and fretting about it when the door opened and the director poked her head around it. "Okay to come in?"

Clara nodded and tried to smile back at her. Holding her breath, she prepared to hear just when she'd be going back home. She could hardly believe her ears, but the words that came out of the boss's mouth were not what she expected.

"Let's give it a few days' rest, then we'll put you on stall-cleaning duty. We have lots of chores that don't require you to be on a horse."

Even mucking out stalls sounded good to her right then. At least she got to stay. And after a few days, there she was doing grunt work, mucking the few stalls for horses needing attention, filling the water troughs, doing pretty much anything that could be done by a person dragging her leg around in a cast. And she also found time each day to write. After a while, she realized she had the whole progression program they'd developed for Girl Scout horseback riding badges down on paper.

Of the many things Clara felt grateful for during her convalescence, a major one was her friends, and sometimes that extended to a friend's parents, as well. Sunny, known as Sue Gibson in life outside camp, was one warm, full-of-fun, delightful person. And no wonder, she thought, when she met Sunny's parents and felt their kindness and thoughtfulness right off the bat.

Then when the Chester accident happened, Sue's mom and dad had taken her in when she had to see doctors in Denver. They wanted her to stay with them, and Mrs. Gibson made sure to cook Clara's favorite foods. She took care beyond that, too, driving Clara to appointments, and had even taught her some new card games.

She could definitely see where Sunny's genial disposition and good sense came from. Clara couldn't have known at the time, but she wouldn't have been surprised that she and Sunny would still be in touch more than five decades later, when they were far into their seventies. In 1957, when they were barely twenty, it was enough for Clara that she had that friendship then. She treasured it.

I could see why when I had the opportunity to meet Sunny, now Sue Bishop, some fifty-eight years after their Flying G days. Clara gave me Sue's contact information and I called, hoping she was still at that number and that she would be willing to talk with me. With a yes on both counts, we arranged to meet at The Market on Denver's Larimer Street. It's a popular lunch spot, and neither of us knew what the other looked like, but somehow we spotted each other right away.

Warm, smiling and lovely, Sue's camp name of Sunny suited her perfectly. We chatted like old friends for a couple of hours, with so much of what Clara had told me coming to life all over again. I was moved by the thought that those young women had come from vastly different backgrounds, had shared experiences out of the ordinary for both and, because of those experiences at that point in their lives, had become lifelong friends. And there Sue and I were, connecting over our mutual friendship with Clara.

Clara's friends. They have always been many and sincere, as they were in this case. As was true with Sunny. Clara credits her friends for helping make the time she was in that cast not such long weeks. And then she was back in the saddle on Chester, taking him over all kinds of ground, trotting, galloping, cantering, walking. But then she realized, with something of a sinking heart, that Chester had turned into the ideal horse, not just for her, but for everybody. She knew that meant she had to give him up. Had it been worth a busted knee, she asked herself. Thinking of the pleasure the girls would get from riding him, her heart told her yes.

Other activities compensated for giving up Chester, such as an occasional weekend at the staff house with some of the other counselors. Aware of the house's history with the property's previous wealthy Russian owners, as a honeymoon cabin for their son and his new wife, she appreciated the chance to be there with friends. She admired the rockwork, the towering fireplace, the beautiful wood, cooking facility and even bunk beds. Everything you need is here, she thought, and what a setting for it to be in.

What a place to be with friends. What a time this was in their lives. She felt so lucky to share it all with these people she cared about. She couldn't help thinking about all the possibilities ahead for all of them. She felt it in her bones. She loved this country. She cherished the camp friendships. Now, she wondered, how was she going to figure out how to live in the Rockies?

1958

I'D BEEN SURPRISED WHEN CLARA TOLD ME SHE AND MARGARET DIDN'T really get to know each other at all that first year. That it was only when they got up to mischief together the second year they were both at the Flying G that they became friends. And they did get up to mischief, perhaps somewhat by happenstance, and it was another of those "slight things" that altered so much that came after.

MARGARET'S FRIEND MAC SUGGESTED SHE APPLY TO BE A GIRL SCOUT camp counselor. Mac had been involved with Girl Scouts for decades, taking groups on all kinds of trips, hiking, camping, backpacking.

Margaret had been happy to assist with as many of those as she could, and she was sure that experience had helped her get this job. That and Mac's recommendation. A person was lucky to get Barbara Macgregor to vouch for her. But Mac was her friend, her buddy. That she was fifteen years older than Margaret meant she had experience and wisdom that Margaret could learn from, more to appreciate.

She'd been really happy to be here last year, although she'd worried that she hadn't known enough about horses. But she must've learned fast enough and done okay because here she was again. She'd had many years of her own scouting, earning numerous badges, all of which she loved—in birding, sailing, botany, among the many. Glad that her Girl Scout troop was one of the rare mariner groups, she took advantage of sailing as a natural part of the Scouts in Oakland. She loved it and all of its elements—the water, wind, seagulls crying overhead, knowing how to set the sails so the boat went where you wanted it to go. A free feeling, and based on her own efforts.

She'd always wished she could've had more experience with horses. As a kid that had been pretty much limited to the occasional pony ride at a birthday party and riding her Uncle Bill's big old workhorse. But last year, she'd made up for some of the lost time, and she'd eaten it up. The Flying G was a great place, complete with mountains, beautiful scenery, fresh air, and new friends. But the horse part had been really exciting. She wished she could always be around horses and was happy to be around them now, and especially to be around them in the Colorado Rockies. She didn't see how it could get any better.

Some of the other staff were back this year, too. Sunny from Denver. Birdy from Kansas. Birdy had helped her out with that cinch early on last year, which had been real nice of her. And she hadn't been pushy or nosey about it at all. Not then, not later. Nice person. Great that Lolly was here again, too. Lolly seemed to her an unlikely name for Delores Villareal, who'd been to Peru on a Fulbright and spoke fluent Spanish, along with some high-class English. But when you got to know her, it fit perfectly. She could talk anybody into anything in any language it seemed, and she was so funny and good-natured on top of it.

As she walked to the lodge for supper one evening, Margaret noticed that after only a few days, she was getting used to the altitude. Because she was always on the move with softball, hiking, and anything else that came along, she knew she was in good shape, but it had surprised her last year that going from sea level to about eight thousand feet could make a difference in her breathing. It hadn't taken long to get over it, though.

Skipping up the lodge steps, she could hear the din inside. People still catching up with each other on the past months almost in tune with the clatter of plates and utensils. As she walked into the dining hall, she saw Jeannene, Lolly, and Birdy chattering away and went over to join them.

"Hey, Punky. Listen to what Lolly's managed to do!" Clara stood aside a bit so Margaret could be part of the small circle.

"It's not such a big deal," Lolly protested. "I just asked the caretaker to give me an old rug and a rocking chair to spiff up my tent a little."

"A rug and furniture! Hell. That's livin'!" Margaret envisioned her Spartan tent with its cot and small box for her clothes. The only place she could rock was on the edge of her cot.

She looked over at Clara and caught a mysterious gleam in her eye. Somehow she recognized it. A tad bit of jealousy? Revenge? Hinting a favors-come-with-with-a-price lesson?

Margaret wasn't quite sure whose idea it was, but she did know the plot she and Clara developed was classic. If they pulled it off, she thought that if there were such a thing, it might even go down in the Camp Book of Records for Best Prank.

Margaret had the feeling that Clara could be as patient as she could herself when it came to the perfect execution of a plan, and that turned out to be true. They waited for days until Lolly took her whole unit of older girls on one of those overnight trekking and camping trips away from the Flying G.

Knowing the coast was clear, that night after work Margaret saw

Clara signal her that it was time to saddle up their horses and ride over to the other camp to Lolly's tent. Since the whole unit was gone, Margaret knew they didn't have to worry about being spotted. Still, they thought it best to work fast, just in case. Margaret took the rocking chair to tie on to her horse, while Clara rolled up the rug and put it on hers. Leading the horses back to the barn, they worked carefully to set the stage just right. Margaret knew Lolly and the girls would be back early the next morning, so timing and set-up had to be just right. She was particular that way, and she was learning her partner-in-prank was, too.

Next morning, Margaret met Clara at the barn to make final preparations. Finishing just in time, Margaret crawled up to her appointed spot and watched Clara find a place where she could take in the whole scene.

As if on cue, Margaret spotted the camp's old pickup coming down the road, little clouds of dust trailing behind. She could see Lolly sitting in the truck's bed, surrounded by the girls. She signaled a "thumbs up" to Clara, who returned the signal with a nod and a big grin. The truck turned in by the barn, and Margaret watched out of the corner of her eye for Lolly's reaction to what she was about to see.

Astonished. Margaret figured that was Lolly's first reaction because she saw Lolly's mouth drop open, her eyes widening till they looked like they might pop out. Then she was pointing up at Margaret, who, for her part, was trying to look completely involved in the book she was holding in front of her as she rocked slowly back and forth in Lolly's rocking chair. And Lolly's carpet was lying across the top of that big old barn, the ends flapping in the breeze.

The girls stared, not knowing if it was okay to laugh or not, but some of them weren't able to stop. Lolly was pointing and screaming in Spanish. And though Margaret didn't know the language, she would've bet her boots Lolly was swearing.

After Lolly calmed down, after she and Clara promised to return the stuff to Lolly's tent, Margaret and Clara had to find a private place so they could bust a gut, get their laughing done. They held their sides, bent over double, laughed and laughed. The whole thing had been so much fun. Margaret, learning that her new friend liked a little drama as much as she did herself, couldn't wait for their next chance.

To Margaret's delight, that next chance came soon, and their target this time happened to be the starchy camp director. Double joy. Margaret wasn't alone in resenting the director's own lack of restrictions in going where she wanted to go and claiming time off when she wanted it. That freedom caused more than a little envy for Margaret and everyone else. So when the woman made plans to go to a special concert at Red Rocks, the beautiful, natural rock amphitheater over near Morrison, Margaret thought it was time something be done. She was pleased that Clara agreed. It wasn't just that the director got to go to the concert. It was that she let everyone else know just how wonderful it was going to be. Margaret and her pal thought there oughta be a little balance in this equation. And she felt sure they were up to the challenge.

Now pretty familiar with that rugged country, Margaret knew it wasn't unusual to find bridges washed out or roads blocked by rockslides or some other of Mother Nature's tricks. And Clara pointed out to her that the shelf road from Deckers to the Flying G was fairly often closed for one reason or another.

Knowing where the art supplies were kept, Margaret suspected everything they needed was there. Well, she thought, we've got the means, the motive and the opportunity. We can't let this one get us by. Plus, she'd won that international poster-making contest, hadn't she? And she knew that Clara's imagination and daring matched hers, so they were set.

When Clara brought in the stiff poster paper she'd backed with plywood, Margaret was ready with her brush and paint. It didn't take her long to complete the task. She stepped back from her work to let Clara admire the bold lettering on the white, easy-to-see paper: BRIDGE OUT!

Margaret chuckled when Clara suggested they post the sign about two miles from the camp in the middle of the road. She and Clara were both gleeful that it had been raining a little off and on all day and evening, making the idea of a bridge out more believable.

Waiting till breakfast the next morning to hear the story was hard, but Margaret knew they couldn't be seen hanging around before that. When she and Clara finally did hear it, they relished every word, the lateness of the hour, how tired the director had been, the slight drizzle soaking her. Margaret especially liked that the woman never even questioned if the bridge was out. When she got to that sign in the wee hours of the morning, she just pulled her car over and parked so she wouldn't be blocking any official or emergency vehicles. Then she hiked the two miles to the camp. Margaret knew Clara was as relieved as she was that she never found out the bridge wasn't out. And even though everybody else knew, nobody squealed on them.

Margaret knew for certain now there was more mischief-making ahead of them, but she thought the stuff with Lolly and the director would probably be their masterpieces. Stealing the director's boots in the middle of the night and running them up the flagpole was small stuff, but it told Margaret, once again, just how much they thought they could get away with anything. And as the summer went on, they did.

But something more important was coming out of that mischief-making, Margaret realized. She thought Clara knew it, too. It was bringing them closer together, and she believed a really good friendship was starting. And so she was way past pleased when Clara invited her to visit in Rago after camp was over.

One thing Margaret knew from being at the Flying G: she loved the mountains. More specifically, she loved the Rockies. Being in the Colorado Rockies had changed something for her for sure. She knew that's where she wanted to be. And she wanted to be around horses. That was another thing she'd learned at the Flying G. She didn't know how she was going to make it happen, but she knew with every bone in her body that she wanted to.

Next thing she knew something transpired that would quite possibly change the direction of her life. She could hardly believe her ears when Clara told her that she, too, wanted to live in the Rockies and raise horses. Margaret didn't know who was more amazed that they shared that dream, Clara or her. Then Clara uttered words that really did change things. She would never forget it. "Well one old-maid school teacher can't afford to do too much, but two old maid school teachers together can do a lot of damage." And Margaret knew that was absolutely true.

A slight thing, a sentence. This one changed the direction of their lives. What luck that was. What very good luck.

2

Homes & Horizons
1958

TAKING IN THE VAST FIELDS OF CORN GROWN TALL IN THE MID-WEST-ern sun, acres and acres of tasseled gold and green swaying in the hot August wind, she thought Kansas could go on forever. Gold-green fields and wide blue sky. Not a cloud to be seen. The horizon as distant as the one over the Pacific Ocean. So many different worlds to know, to see. Or so I imagine Margaret thinking as Mrs. Reida drove her and Clara away from the Flying G Ranch and on home across those wide-open spaces that late summer of 1958.

The visit to the Reidas old home place was a big deal for her, because of her friendship with Clara, because of their shared hopes and dreams. And she didn't know it then, but she would have discoveries about the farm, about living close to the land, that would contribute to, and certainly confirm, the shaping of her life. Trying to put myself in her shoes and in her mind, I wanted to see and feel that visit. Here's how I think it might have gone.

As they drove across the flat land, Clara filled her in on farming, when the spring wheat was planted, April through May, she heard her say, and it was harvested about a month ago, so some of the fields were getting prepared for the winter wheat crop. Clara's family farmed mostly winter wheat, along with a grain sorghum called milo, an occasional cane crop, and a little alfalfa. But all those acres and acres of corn other farmers grew wouldn't be harvested for another few weeks. This was all new to her. Not much farming in Oakland, another world entirely.

She liked seeing new places, lapped up learning new things. Especially if it had to do with the outdoors. And she liked knowing more about Clara and the place she came from. She wanted to see this farm on which Clara baled hay, broke horses, milked cows, plowed fields, fed chickens. And she really looked forward to meeting others in her friend's family, although she couldn't help wondering if they'd think she was okay. That she was capable of doing things, not just a big-city girl. Would she fit in?

They drove through Kingman, a picturesque town with its wide brick streets and stately church steeples, and she knew they were just a short drive from Rago and then to the Reida farm. Seeing the train tracks and a self-propelled rail car, the Doodlebug, coming down toward them reminded her of the stories Clara had told about it. How it was used for lines that had fewer passengers. And especially how her dad used to race it in their car, the family all piled in, laughing and shouting, the car kicking up clouds of dust. Clara had raced it, too, on Queen, her well-loved buckskin. Margaret liked that Queen could outrun it in a burst of speed, even if the Doodlebug would win in the end.

Meeting Clara's mother when she came to pick them up at the Flying G felt a little bit like coming home, she was so welcoming, so glad to meet Margaret, calling her Punky right off the bat, the nickname her father had given her as a kid and that everyone now called her. She looked forward to meeting the others, oldest brother Gale, who was about fifteen years older than Clara and who lived nearby. Also close by was Ray, five years younger than Clara, the youngest of the five. Margaret knew seventeen-years-older Zelda and her family lived out of state, and wouldn't likely be around. She'd have to meet that sister another time. But she did hope to see Virginia, who also was married and had family, but lived within driving distance.

Riding along, Margaret listened to and sometimes joined in the lively chit chat, answering questions about the trip, camp, herself. But she didn't want to miss seeing the farms and fields, her eyes always moving to look out the window. She knew when they drove down through the creek they were at the home place Clara had told her so much about. Warming immediately to the old house sitting there on its many acres of farmland, she also welcomed the sight of the windmill standing nearby, the dogs, chickens, and of course, the horses, all familiar from Clara's stories.

Margaret settled into the visit easily enough. Not hard with such a hospitable family. Being around Mrs. Reida, hearing more about Clara's father who died when Clara was so young, getting to know some of Clara's brothers and sisters, cousins, nieces, nephews, all of this was fascinating. She could see where Clara's sunny disposition came from. Her steadiness, too.

She pitched in with the chores, feeding those chickens, pigs, cows, and horses, helping in the kitchen, and went riding with Clara. Watching Ray turning the dirt for new crops fascinated her so much, she took picture after picture, using almost a whole roll of film in only a few days.

She and Clara rode horses all over that farm, across all the land Rudolph, Clara's grandfather, had divided up to give each of his four sons and three daughters their own farms. Clara had guessed they were no less than half a section, about three hundred twenty acres each. And then Clara's father, Arnold, had done the same, five kids—two sons and three daughters, five farms, only these were smaller parcels, maybe more like farmettes, around eighty acres. It amazed her that someone would do that. Could do that. Rudolph had emigrated here from Austria, just like her own father's family had come to America from somewhere in Italy. But she reckoned their lives had taken very different tacks because her father hadn't had any land to leave his two daughters.

On horseback they saw Hopewell Elementary School, the little one-room schoolhouse Clara and her siblings had gone to. Margaret could picture little grade-school Clara riding a big horse to school, come rain or shine. She admired Clara's ability with horses. She wished she'd grown up with them the way Clara had, wished she knew how to handle and work with them with such skill. Clara was so natural with them, like they were a part of her. Even though she'd learned a lot from Clara and from being at the Flying G, she knew she was far from being the natural her friend was.

They saw pretty much all the places Clara had told her about, plus a few. It all made her happy. Hot in Kansas in August, though that didn't bother her so much, but the wind took a little more getting used to. Somehow, though, fresh lemonade or ice-cold watermelon made it all seem just fine.

When some of the family dropped by, maybe Gale who lived just over the hill, or nearby Virginia, Margaret saw that the conversation could get pretty spirited. Listening to family stories, she loved the way the Reidas all pitched in with prompts and different parts of the tale.

"Remember when Gale came back from the war?"

"Oh, my. What a surprise, almost a shock that was."

"Well, he'd been off in Europe right in the thick of the fighting. And although we knew he was coming, we sure didn't know when. He'd been good about writing, but we hadn't seen him in four years."

"Margaret, have you heard this one?" She heard Mrs. Reida sigh deeply.

Margaret shook her head and leaned forward, ready to listen as Clara took it from there.

"Mom, Virginia, and I were out milking the cows, just coming back in. Mom was carrying two pails full of fresh milk. All of a sudden, she started whirling those pails up and around over her shoulders, just whirling like crazy! Those pails were going around so fast they didn't spill a drop of milk. Then she let go and they sailed through the air, the milk flying out in a perfect arc. Virginia let out a whoop and a yell. That's when I realized that man walking toward us was Gale."

Margaret did know that Gale had been in the war, and that it had been as hard on him as it'd been on so many others. She knew he suffered still from the awfulness and horror of it. Somehow knowing this made the story that much more moving to her, but she didn't say so. Clara had told her, too, that Gale had gotten home not long before their father died. It made her feel a little better knowing Mr. Reida had been able to see his son before he passed. Mr. Reida had only been forty-eight.

Clara had talked to her pretty often about her father, how she felt his influence still, even though she'd been only eight years old when he died. That was sure something they had in common. Losing their dads so young. Clara'd told her about his reputation as an honest man, a person with a lot of integrity, someone whose handshake meant everything, the way it was for her dad's dad. Sounded like father and son were a lot alike. Clara had told her, "With Dad if your word wasn't good, then you weren't good. Period. That's all there was to it. And if you couldn't be trusted, you couldn't be worthy of anything. If you told a lie … you were dead meat!"

Margaret couldn't help but wonder if Clara had known this last part first-hand. But when she thought about it, she decided probably not. Clara was just like her dad and granddad herself. About as straightforward as they come. Trustworthy, reliable. Warm-hearted, but no pushover.

At Sunday dinner Margaret counted more people than she had in her whole family, at least family she knew of. The laughing, kidding around, and genuine caring there made her think about home. She and her stepfather could hardly stand each other. Not much hope of them ever really enjoying each other's company. And that set kind of a tone most of the time, although there were the rare times they could get past that.

And there at Clara's, it wasn't just who was sitting around the table, the family and the caring. It was what was on the table, too. Green beans, tomatoes, radishes, all fresh from the garden. Deviled eggs, with eggs straight from the chickens she'd fed herself. Pork chops from one of the Reidas' own pigs. Newly baked bread and pies. Everything wonderful tasting. Margaret liked to cook, and she liked eating good cooking. All these home-grown vegetables and other things from the farm tickled her taste buds, and they inspired her. She told herself that when she and Clara really did get that ranch, she was going to make sure she had a big garden, fresh eggs and meat. She made that vow to herself, and she was gonna keep it.

When the talk turned to music, Margaret tuned in more closely. She knew this was something dear to Clara's heart, and she knew how beautifully her friend could sing. Mrs. Reida was saying, "Arnold could play any instrument he picked up. But he stuck mainly with stringed instruments and especially that fiddle that he learned to play when the family band needed a fiddler. The one who'd been with them died, and they wanted Arnold to fill in. He said, 'Maudie, I'll get a fiddle and learn to play it if you learn the harmonica.'"

When Ray said, "And you did, didn't you, Mom? Maybe you should play for us now," Margaret hoped Mrs. Reida would do that. But she just smiled.

A family band? Her curiosity tweaked, Margaret asked, "What else did people play?"

"Accordion, piano, tub drum, along with Mom's harmonica and Dad's fiddle," Virginia told her. "It was mostly our aunts and uncles. They played for dances and just for fun. They were pretty popular around here."

Mrs. Reida explained to her that they had to make their own music in those days, that the only radio they had then was battery operated.

Jumping in to describe for her just what went in to listening to that radio, Clara explained, "They charged the battery with a little wind charger, as they called it. It was a little bitty windmill out on the machine shed. Dad would run out there with the battery and hook it on the charger. The wind would charge one while we were listening to another already charged."

Margaret felt her own battery charging. Living close to the land like this, being able to harness that wind to make things function. Hard work, yes, but being more independent, self-sufficient. This appealed to every part of her.

As for family, she sure didn't have a sense of her roots like Clara did. Clara knew just where her grandfather came from, and even before that. To know that Rudolph had been in seminary but had become disillusioned with the Church. To understand about the Austrian Empire, that their family was from a part of it that was known as Moravia, Bohemia. That Granddad Rudolph Reida came to this country with two of his brothers because they didn't want to be recruited into the Emperor's Army.

He'd become a U.S. citizen on July 11, 1892 and moved to Kansas in 1893 where he met Mary Thiel, a Hungarian immigrant in 1894. All this seemed like gold to her. Family gold. Not to mention a good history lesson. She didn't know much about these things, and she thought they were exciting. They were all real things, all connected to people she now knew and cared about.

These were worlds beyond the Kansas or Oakland world and knowing about them made being there in Rago, Kansas even richer. She thought about the Kansas horizon, and that of Oakland, and on to the Pacific. How amazing it was that all this was now in her life because of meeting Clara at Girl Scout camp. Because she and Clara had made all that mischief, had become friends, kind of like sisters, and maybe one day they'd really be business partners in that ranch. She sure hoped so. Another world, another horizon.

1963

I SUSPECT EACH OF THE SEVERAL VISITS MARGARET MADE TO KANSAS to see Clara and family further confirmed and strengthened those two young women's resolve to have their own ranch. Then came the chance for Clara to go west. With the school year at an end, she would take the train to Oakland, meet Margaret's family and help her move to Kansas. I wanted to take that trip with her, so in my mind's eye, I did.

SHE STILL FOUND IT HARD TO BELIEVE, EVEN AFTER A DAY AND NIGHT traveling west on the Santa Fe Chief, that she was on her way to California. On her way to visit Margaret and, at long last, meet her family—her mom, Dorothy, stepdad Mike, Aunt Marg and her husband Darrell. It wasn't a big sprawling family like the Reidas, but a more compact one. Even more compact since Margaret's sister, Louise, had died only a couple of years ago. That thought saddened her.

Recalling the cancer Louise suffered, and the urgent call that came during one of Margaret's Rago visits, she mused about the long dread-filled drive home to Oakland Margaret had had to make. It must have been doubly hard driving through this seemingly empty landscape with such fear and emptiness inside her gut. The urgency was all too real, Louise died very shortly after Margaret got there. August 10, 1961.

Losing her father when she was only eleven or so to cancer, then Louise as a young adult were two heavy blows, travesties her friend rarely talked about, but she knew they were there inside her somewhere. How could they not be?

But now Clara would meet the rest of the family, just as Margaret had met hers, visiting every summer, further deepening the bonds with her family each time. She hoped Margaret's family would like her, too.

Pleased about the plan for Margaret to drive back to Kansas, Clara was particularly happy that they'd both be teaching in Kansas in the upcoming school year, and they'd be making preparations to find that ranch in Colorado. This would be a big Step One, followed by Step Two of saving money, and building up their herd.

Appaloosa horses were what they wanted to breed, and she knew Margaret was as excited as she was about it. Clara had gotten hooked on the crazy color patterns of Appaloosas from pictures she'd seen. She hadn't even seen a live one at the time. Then someone bet her a steak dinner that she couldn't get any Apps out of the mares she already had. The person didn't know she'd selected the mares with characteristics based on some very good advice from an old horseman. Four out of five of the first ones she bred had color, meaning the characteristic Appaloosa spots, and the other one changed to color. She won a steak dinner, and her appreciation of Appaloosas only got stronger.

Step Three would be finding the ranch, and that would come in due course. In the meantime, they would live on the old home place with her mom. Now that she was heading west, farther west than she'd ever been, she felt with all her heart that their dream would become a reality. Her spine tingled with anticipation.

She was glad her friend Frances had wanted to make this trip with her. It made the travel a lot more fun, especially since it all was such a new experience, an adventure. They'd boarded at Harper, only a few miles from home and now they were more than half way to Oakland. And if she couldn't believe she was heading west, had come through long expanses of four states already, something else that stretched her credulity was how vast the country was. The endless Arizona desert she looked out across, and the varying landscapes that had come in between in Kansas, southeastern Colorado, New Mexico, now this. Her eyes ached from looking so far. In a whole lot of the country there was so much land and so few trees. The land went on and on. Light brown, dark brown, kind of a shadowy purple.

But it wasn't all the same. Punctuating the flatness, interesting formations rose up into the seeming emptiness. She saw a few houses here and there, but no crops. It seemed sparse, but beautiful, and it was such a contrast to where she'd spent her life. She felt though it was strange, it held its own beauty.

Not wanting to miss anything, she sat with Frances in the observation car where they spent most of the daylight hours. That Frances Zimmerman. What a good friend and easy-going traveling companion. She was glad she'd gotten to know her better right after she'd started teaching at Harper High School a couple years ago. Their families had known each other forever, but she and Frances had really become friends through work.

Frances was the one who'd gotten her involved in the professional women's organization. It wasn't her type of thing at all, but she'd stuck with it for a while because of Frances. They'd gone to meetings and also made up skits together about Nike, the ancient Greek winged goddess of victory, who was supposed to be their guide. Frances got right into writing those skits with her, and if nobody else thought them funny, she and Frances sure did. Sometimes she had a hard time not hooting out loud at some of the chants, called responses, and other rituals. She thought all of those women were really nice, but this kind of organization and these rituals just weren't her thing.

Now as she and Frances watched the passing landscape, she could hear the twelve-year-old boys as they came into the car and toward them.

Those kids weren't accustomed to long hours in confined quarters, and they'd already had plenty of that. To entertain them, and herself, she'd been teasing them a lot and teaching them fun songs, not the inappropriate ones she'd learned at college, but old ones like "You Are My Sunshine" and "Little Brown Jug." Now they were coming back for more.

"Hey, Clara," she heard one of them call. "You promised to teach us how to sing rounds. We're ready!"

She saw how intent the boys were as they plopped themselves down around her and Frances, some on the seats, others on the floor, all ten pairs of eyes on her.

"Okay. Frances and I will show you how it's done. Then we'll pair you off and you can take it from there."

The boys did just that, listening attentively as she and Frances sang a few rounds, then eagerly taking it up themselves. They practiced a few times before she watched them race off to entertain other travelers. From the far side of the car Clara soon heard young voices singing in overlapping refrains, "Row, row, row your boat, Gently down the stream ... " followed by fellow passengers laughing and clapping. She didn't know who was having more fun, the kids, the other travelers, or her.

She'd welcomed the fun with the boys. Truth was, despite the interesting country, she wasn't used to being confined that long herself. She liked action, activity, and was glad when the train pulled into the station and she and Frances found their way into the bustling, crowded terminal. Sure enough, there was Margaret waiting for them. That friendly, familiar face in the sea of strangers helped her get her feet back on the ground and eased the anxiety about being in such a different place. She really hoped she wouldn't do something stupid in this place that was poles apart from her own.

Weaving through the heavy traffic in her 1956 Chevy, Margaret headed them toward her Oakland home on San Joaquin Boulevard, a feat that impressed Clara no end. Margaret pointed out various landmarks, and the one that stood out for Clara was the huge Mormon Temple just below her house. She was all agog. She thought it beautiful, sitting there on its magnificent grounds and framed by fountains, all of it overlooking the Bay Area. Wishing she could see the inside, Margaret reminded her she was an outsider, and that just wasn't going to happen.

Meeting Dorothy, Margaret's mom, and Mike, her stepfather, seemed all very smooth and natural, thank goodness. They seemed so open and accommodating, as were Margaret's Aunt Marg and Uncle Darrell. Everybody nice and down to earth, which was good since she felt a little bit like an alien from outer space. And there was Smokey, the Weimaraner, and Duffy, Margaret's cairn terrier. Spunky little dickens, and as clever as Margaret had said he was.

Oakland and San Francisco astonished her. She'd never seen anything like it. Of course, she was expecting a city, something along the lines of Kansas City, which seemed plenty big to her. But San Francisco and Oakland seem to be stopped only by large bodies of water. And they were intense. Tall buildings everywhere, streets jammed with cars, buses, trolleys, pedestrians, horns honking, music drifting out of bars, homes, people dressed in every kind of clothing you could imagine, and every kind of culture you could imagine. In San Francisco, those up and down streets with tall houses built all the way up and down boggled her mind.

Margaret took her and Frances to every kind of place imaginable, except, of course, the Mormon Temple. She even drove them up the coast to Bodega Bay, where the terrifying new Alfred Hitchcock movie, *The Birds*, had been set. Riding along, looking out at the ocean, it seemed to her that the world just went on forever. The ocean's mist seemed to make the water fade into the sky. It was all so big, endless. The occasional freighter, made small by the vast ocean, mirrored the smallness she felt in that ocean's presence. Peacefulness, too.

She thought the variety of experiences to be had were astonishing. Those massive and beautiful Bay and Golden Gate Bridges wouldn't be leaving her mind for a while. And the ocean and Bodega Bay were quite a contrast to their trip to a piano bar. Hard to believe this Midwestern, Bible-belt girl was actually going into a bar. But Mike had asked them to meet him at this place he liked particularly well, and as a houseguest, she felt she should go. She also felt curious. So there she was with Frances and Margaret, off to a bar.

She knew they were supposed to time it to meet Mike after he got off work, which was doing something with court records for the Oakland Police Department. She also knew that he sometimes worked undercover in special cases. That Mike had been struck by polio as a child and now had to use two crutches aided his undercover work. Nobody believed a handicapped person could be with the police. That's what made him so good at it. Nobody suspected. And he rarely talked about it to anyone.

Walking through Jack London square and shivering a bit in the cool Bay Area evening, they arrived at the bar right on time. Margaret and Frances went in first, Clara following closely. She hardly had time to take in the soft lighting, the leather booths, the long marble bar and high-backed barstools when the first notes burst from the black grand piano angled in the center of the room. Then a clear, sonorous voice sang out, "I'm going to Kansas City, Kansas City here I come ... " with everyone in the bar joining in after the first few words. Mike included. Caught completely unawares, Clara laughed out loud, and then Frances with her, both clapping their hands along with Margaret. The thought that Mike had set it all up seeped in through her surprise. What fun this was. And her, in a bar!

After hearing about them for years, Clara enjoyed meeting Margaret's friends, some from school, some who taught at the same inner-city school she did, others who were or had been neighbors. There was another Clara, Clara Huillade, and Drew, Evie, and Mac and her housemate, Phyllis, whom everyone called Phyl. She remembered that Mac and Phyl were examples of the single women Margaret knew who'd put their resources together to buy a home. In some cases, three or four women went in together. It sure made for a better place to live, especially in a city where everything seemed unusually expensive. Most importantly, she knew Margaret had helped Mac on numerous school and Girl Scout camping trips, and Mac had been helpful in Margaret's going to the Flying G in the first place. Otherwise, Margaret and Clara would've never even met.

Knowing how much Margaret enjoyed hearing the stories her family and friends told when she had been in Kansas several summers in a row, Clara took pleasure in knowing now it was her turn to hear about Margaret. And she wasn't disappointed.

"Hey, Punky, just how many camping trips have you and Mac taken kids on?" someone asked.

"Didn't count 'em," Margaret said.

"Okay, so where have you gone?"

"All over the mountains, when I'm wasn't working at Drug King for Aunt Marg. Mac arranged trips in the Sierras, Yosemite, the Oakland and Berkeley Hills, and I was happy to go along and help. We were in most of California's best places. "

"And now?"

"I don't get to do as much now," Margaret shook her head. "But I do want my students to know more than what a city offers. These kids have had tough lives, and they love it. That's a pretty good incentive."

Clara had heard Margaret talk about her hands-on, out-of-the ordi-nary approaches to whatever she taught, and how she just expected the kids to learn. And apparently, they did. Clara understood this because she felt much the same way about teaching. Her kids were mostly rural farm kids, but she expected a lot from them, gave them the support they needed, and they delivered. Margaret's students led very different lives, and she knew from what Mac and others said that Margaret went out of her way to make sure those kids had a range and depth of experience that was all too rare in their schooling, and in their lives in general.

Being in nature was key to Margaret. Clara understood how much she wanted those kids to know more than the city offered. That wasn't easy, but she wanted them to have the kind of experiences she'd held dear with her father, experiences that had helped shaped who she was.

She thought it was just plain wonderful that Margaret and Mac took the kids on backpacking trips in territory those young people wouldn't have known otherwise, under stars they wouldn't have seen through city lights, in mountain air they couldn't have breathed in a car-studded metropolis.

Now she was hearing about how Margaret had carried on what Mac had taught her, organizing things so the kids themselves would pack in, set up camp, cook, clean up, and generally learn to work together, each doing their part. There they found something beyond themselves, beyond the difficulties of everyday life, something to inspire and help cultivate their sense of a larger world.

And she'd even had a chance to talk with Mac about some of her own adventures. No wonder Mac had been such an influence and inspiration for Margaret. Absolutely nothing stopped her. Now nothing was going to stop Clara from learning more about this smart, tough, yet somehow genteel Barbara Macgregor.

To Clara, Mac's philosophy seemed to be that you have to do what you want because you don't know how long you have to do it. It sure made sense to her. But it amazed Clara just what form that philosophy had taken in Mac's life.

From hitchhiking alone through Alaska—her mother thought she was with a friend, but the friend dropped out at the last minute—to bicycling from Oakland to San Diego, going to New York right out of university—and working in a laboratory with a future Nobel Laureate—to being a scout leader and YMCA leader, to making trips co-educational, it seemed to Clara that Mac didn't even recognize the word "obstacle."

She'd even taken kids on trips overseas. First to Western Europe, and as Mac said, "on a nickel and a dime. The kids earned money for the trips, and we didn't really live very high in the world, but we saw the world, and we walked the world, we bicycled through the world. We rented horses, and then we bought our own bicycles."

Thrilled to hear about these explorations, Clara asked for and got more. "Western Europe first, then the next year other parts of Europe. We've been to the Philippines and several countries in the Middle East. For next year we're planning a two-month round-the-world trip with about ninety-five kids and five group leaders. It will include Japan, India,

Pakistan, Nepal, Vietnam and more. We'll stay mostly in youth hostels as we've been doing. No chance to overeat doing that!"

When Clara had a chance to talk with Frances about what they'd heard, she said, "Talk about Nike. I think we've been in the room with a real live winged goddess whose victory is living just as she wants to live. And helping kids see just how big life can be. Now that's something worth paying attention to."

The time was approaching now for a little more travel on Clara's part, and although it wasn't across the ocean, it was half a continent back to Rago, Kansas. What a great time she and Frances had had here. It might not be the place Clara wanted to live, but she was grateful for the experiences she'd had in this city and for the people she'd met. She wouldn't forget any of it or them and she made sure they all knew they'd be welcome to visit when she and Margaret had their ranch.

Along with Jon, a young teen-aged great-nephew of Mike's who wanted to see the country, Clara, Margaret, and Frances, climbed into Margaret's Chevy and set off on their journey. This time the view was even more close-up, making the vastness seem that much greater. And hotter. Crossing the desert, she thought surely they would melt. It was so hot that she couldn't even handle the change in her wallet when they stopped for a cold soda.

But that didn't last forever. They drove over mountains, through canyons, across prairies, and on to the golden-green fields of Kansas. Happy with the adventures she'd had, the sights she'd seen, and especially the people she'd met, she sighed deeply when they drove through the creek and up to the house with the old windmill still standing against that smaller horizon of home.

THEY HAD TRAVERSED THE GREAT EXPANSE FROM CALIFORNIA COASTAL cities to the wheat fields of Kansas. They had been in each other's homes and had met each other's welcoming families and friends, all of which served to deepened their understanding of each other and further strengthen their friendship. The two friends, intentional sisters, and future business partners now settled into the work at hand. They would both be teaching in Kansas. They would save their money, begin building their herd, that crucial Step Two toward making their dream a reality. Kansas would be their temporary home. The ranch was on the horizon.

3

Waking Up and Following a Dream
1963 – 1965

WHEN CLARA LEFT FOR CALIFORNIA, SHE WAS ALSO LEAVING Harper High School where she'd taught the past two years. And prior to that, she taught three semesters in Chislom Trail Junior High in Wichita, Kansas. Being at Harper High had been good because it was closer to home and a high school, a better fit for her teacher preparation.

After only two years at Harper High, imagine the reaction of this modest, hardworking, full-of-life young woman when she saw the article in the school newspaper dedicating the issue to her.

> We, the 1963 *Herald* Staff wish to dedicate this Senior issue to our sponsor, Miss Clara Mary Reida. Besides sponsoring the *Herald*, she has sponsored the yearbook, *Bearcat*, coached the junior and senior plays, managed the SKL Speech Festival and coached speech arts contestants. When she's not occupied by all this, Miss Reida teaches three English III classes, an English IV class, and speech and journalism. Despite this busy schedule she still has time to listen to our gripes and problems. We know when she's arrived at school because we can see her black and white Scout "Tonto" parked in front of the high school.
>
> When her long day at school is finished, she hops into "Tonto" and drives home to her mom and her horses. She then spends a quiet evening grading papers, taking care of the animals, and doing the usual farm chores.
>
> Miss Reida is loved by all her students. She has a warm personality and a sunny smile for all. Her pet peeve is her mother singing "No Letter Today." Her favorite color is blue; as to her favorite food, she just enjoys eating. Her hobby is raising Appaloosa horses; and she just enjoys life in general.
>
> To this wonderful person, with love and heart-felt thanks, we dedicate this issue of the *Herald*.[1]

---

1 *The Harper Herald*. Harper, Kansas: Harper High School. Monday, May 20, 1963, XXVIII, No. 9, 1.

IT WAS QUITE A SEND-OFF ON THAT CALIFORNIA TRIP, AND ALSO A SEND-off into her next two years of teaching at Kingman High school. There she again sponsored clubs and taught English. And in fact, her second year of teaching American Literature at Kingman would play a central role in what would happen next.

Margaret taught elementary grades at Adams School, also sponsoring many extra-curricular activities, including art and sports events. They both made deep impressions on their students. And in Clara's case, those impressions boomeranged to spur the two of them into action.

Sure, they had a plan and had taken Step Two toward it with Margaret's moving to Rago. They were gradually acquiring Appaloosas, keeping them on the farm. They were saving money. The dream of a ranch was very much intact, but it was still in the dream category.

They talked about it a lot. Talking, thinking, planning substituted for action. That is, until Clara's students, after two years of learning Emerson and Thoreau from her had heard enough of their dreams.

"Ms. Reida, you're always teaching what Emerson says and Thoreau says about following your dreams and living your dreams. So when are you gonna go to Colorado?"

Those students knew *Walden*. Clara had taught them well.

> ...[I]f one advances confidently in the direction of his dreams, and endeavors to live the life which he has imagined, he will meet with a success unexpected in common hours ... If you have built castles in the air, your work need not be lost; that is where they should be. Now put the foundations under them.[2]

"Well, that's a good question," she said as more of Thoreau's words echoed in her mind, "It is remarkable how easily and insensibly we fall into a particular route, and make a beaten track for ourselves."[3]

Realization; awakening comes in many ways, sometimes the least expected. "Life is a series of surprises," says Emerson.

The one thing which we seek with insatiable desire is to forget

---

2 Henry D. Thoreau. *Walden, The Works of Henry D. Thoreau*. New York: Thomas Y. Crowell Co., 1940, 427.
3 Ibid, 426

ourselves, to be surprised out of our propriety, to lose our sempiternal memory, and to do something without knowing how or why; in short, to draw a new circle. Nothing great was ever achieved without enthusiasm.[4]

Following one's dreams, getting off the beaten path, and doing so with enthusiasm. The students' questions had indeed "surprised them out of [their] propriety." They would begin their search for a ranch.

Still they believed the search would take time, and time was needed to save enough money. In the mid-1960s, loans for women were rare. They'd give themselves a couple more years teaching in Kansas, save their money, and prepare for the drawing of that new circle. But the new circle was closer than they thought.

---

4 Ralph Waldo Emerson. "Circles," *The Works of Ralph Waldo Emerson*. New York: Tudor Publishing Company, 1930, 20.

A Ranch of Their Own
1965

"Sure, going to the Girl Scout camp and meeting Clara were big steps, but it was buying the ranch and moving to Colorado that started Punky's life." Mac's ninety-year-old voice came through on speakerphone clearly and vigorously. She spoke from Oakland, California. I listened in Boulder, Colorado, entranced by this magnetic woman who'd known Margaret longer than anyone alive, from her late teens till the end, more than five decades. Mac's assessment added yet another layer to the already rich account Clara had been sharing. My brain began sorting this nugget into the mix, conjuring up just how that transitional and transformational time might have played out.

Moved to action by Clara's students, Margaret and Clara pounced on their upcoming spring break, March, 1965, as an opportunity to begin their search. Yes, it was going to take time to find a place, but the kids were right, they needed to start looking, start actively building the foundation for that dream. It wasn't going to build itself.

Digging into their homework, they began figuring out guidelines for themselves. Number one was they ought to be near a city that would likely need teachers. Number two involved cost of living. No matter how much they would be able to save in the next few years, buying a ranch and keeping it running would take money. They weren't kidding themselves about that.

Given those factors, they narrowed the search to the area around Pueblo. With a population around 93,000, Pueblo was large enough to offer teaching opportunities, and it would be less expensive to live near than Denver or Colorado Springs. It was a down-to-earth, working-gal kind of place. Next step was to find a realtor who knew the surrounding rural areas, areas where a ranch of, say eighty to one hundred sixty acres might be waiting for them. Howard Morris reputedly knew the large and sparsely populated area well. They called and set a time to meet.

Margaret liked Howard, and she could tell from their easy banter that Clara did, too. They were grateful that he drove them all around everywhere so they could get a sense of the area. Not many ranches for sale, at least not ones in their size-and-price range, but they were getting a good look at the country, which varied greatly. Sitting at the confluence of the Arkansas River and Fountain Creek in semi-arid country, they learned that Pueblo was in what some called the "banana belt." The city itself sat on a plain, which extended east and south. North and west the country grew more mountainous. If some property were to open up, they would have a better sense of how it would suit them in terms of size, affordability and landscape.

One ranch they looked at impressed Margaret no end. Clara, too. Perched on mountainsides, it seemed straight up and down. Yeah, they both thought looking at the long, narrow cleavages at the foot of significant rises, it was beautiful. "But," Margaret said, "A rancher could starve to death trying to ranch here."

Driving west on highway 96 into Custer County and the Wet Mountains, they stopped by Howard's own newly acquired ranch, with its old log house and wooden outbuildings. That house was definitely picturesque in a homestead kind of way, sitting at an altitude of nine thousand feet, surrounded by mountains, and beautiful meadows, too.

Still laughing about their reaction to the up-and-down ranch, Howard teased, "Lucky for you, it's not for sale! I'm no flatlander, and I'm gonna be spending some good time up here."

That he would spend some good time there, Margaret easily believed. It was a beautiful alpine area, even the little they could see, with aspen stands mixed in with evergreen, and that long meadow running alongside the two-lane highway that led to Westcliffe, some fourteen miles west. The air crisp and clean, the sky a crystallized blue, and few other ranches or homes nearby. Not too surprising since she'd heard Custer County was Colorado's least populated county. Yep, the ranch was a beauty, but not for them, not just starting out, not being familiar with this climate and terrain. Not to mention money and the need to continue teaching while starting up a ranch. Good thing it wasn't for sale.

Leaving the mountains and heading back to Kansas Margaret thought of how she and Clara had talked about what they expected from this scouting trip, that this was only their first look for actual ranches, or at least the area where possibilities might lie. She wasn't disappointed in not finding *the* ranch, but did she feel good they'd begun the search. She didn't expect they would find *it* on this first look. Would've been surprised if they had. Again she voiced the thoughts they'd talked about repeatedly. It was comforting to say them out loud. "It's good to have stuck our toes in the water, and not only to please your students. Now that we've seen some of Pueblo and the area and know Howard, when something comes up, we'll have an idea of what he's talking about."

When Clara smiled and nodded her agreement, Margaret added, reassuring herself, "And there's no hurry. We still need to save more and keep building a herd."

Back at work, the flurry of the final quarter of the school year consumed them. One evening, in the midst of paper grading, they got a call. It was Howard.

"Guess I'm having a heart problem. My doctor says it's serious. He's informed me that I can't even play at the altitude my ranch is. No oxygen. Doesn't like the idea of me being there at all."

Margaret could feel her own heart racing as she shared the phone with Clara and heard Howard's astonishing words coming down the line. He went on. "If you'd like to buy that place, I'll make it possible. I'll take a second mortgage myself, and you can take over the first."

Two pairs of eyes widened and looked at each other. Two mouths dropped open. Although the call and the offer surprised Margaret mightily, it didn't surprise her that she and Clara had exactly the same response. They looked at each other as they hung up the phone. "What do we have to lose?" they asked, almost in unison, laughing in amazed delight. This was manna indeed, and they weren't going to let it melt away.

Nodding wholeheartedly and grinning from ear to ear, Margaret encouraged Clara as her pal listed other supporting factors. "We can get our Colorado teaching licenses, so we can find jobs there. I have several head of horses, and you've got a couple of your own. Then there are a few we own together. Seems to me we can call that a herd."

A quick and excited trip back to Colorado found them making a down payment and seeing more of the place they'd only glimpsed earlier. The place they were buying. A four-hundred-eighty-acre ranch. The more they saw, the more they fell in love with it, despite the growing realization there was a whole lot of hard work ahead of them.

That Howard made it possible for them to buy the ranch left Margaret in awe, and she knew Clara felt the same. They couldn't have done it without Howard's bighearted financial arrangement. They knew their chances as women for a significant mortgage were small to nil. What they didn't know was that twelve years into the future, in 1974, the Equal Credit Opportunity Act would be passed making such gender discrimination illegal. But that wasn't the case in 1965, and they would consider themselves lucky on several occasions when unexpected and creative financing dropped in their laps.

When Margaret considered how Howard's kindness and generosity hadn't stopped with finances, her respect and esteem for him grew even more. He'd taken them to Florence to meet the superintendent of schools who, upon hearing about their credentials and experience, told them they had oral contracts for jobs. Margaret was ready to dance a jig when he told them to call when they got back in June to sign written contracts. This was perfect, Margaret thought. Florence was closer than Pueblo, a little more than a half-hour drive in good weather. How much better could it get?

In early June, as soon as school was out they were back on U.S. Highway 50, on their way west and eager to begin the work. Taking her shift on the four-hundred-fifty-mile drive, Margaret mused on the rapid turn of events. Even thinking about it made her head spin. Here they were actually driving to their ranch, their pickup packed with supplies for their first big task, cleaning the house and making it livable. Not "the house," but "their house." She almost had to pinch herself. To bring herself back to earth, she thought about what they'd brought— bedding, towels, dishes, pots, pans. The essentials. Listing the inventory of the few things in the house they could use, she thought of the old beds upstairs, the well-used oak table in the kitchen, a wood-burning cook stove. Yes, these were things they could see, touch, use. They were real.

Stepping into the little old cabin felt like stepping back in time. Built in 1883, it had three small rooms downstairs, and three up a tricky little staircase. Margaret loved it as it was, but she agreed with Clara that over time they could make it more livable. She was ready and willing to try out the carpentry skills she already had, and also learn a whole lot more. But for now, they'd just have to attend to the basics. That would keep them plenty busy.

Along with the house, they had an outdoor toilet, a tiny barn, a building that had been called a coal house, and a few little out-buildings they would use for chicken houses, along with their four-hundred-eighty acres of land, much of which they still hadn't seen. They'd have to have horses to do that. And they'd have to get some fences up to have their horses here. Margaret was glad they'd decided to get the living quarters in shape before bringing the small herd and more stuff out. This was work enough.

No running water or electricity, but they found people to work on those two projects right away. For those first few weeks they carried their water from the spring back to the house, like the old-timers did, loving every minute of it. They'd stepped into their dream, full of promise, surrounded by beauty, imbued with challenge for these two energetic, hopeful young women. Not many women had had the opportunity or resources to have a ranch on their own. That thought daunted neither of them. It didn't enter their minds what they were doing was all that unusual, that they were pioneers. But not too far down the road, they would learn that a whole lot of people were betting these two pioneers wouldn't succeed. They were, after all, only women. Completely unaware that questions would be raised, they applied themselves to the immediate tasks in front of them. One of those was signing those teaching contracts.

Driving down the canyon, over Hardscrabble Pass, across the prairie and into Florence, Margaret again marveled at how within the twenty-five-mile trip, the landscape showed so much variety, and several thousand feet difference in altitude. She would get to see this variety every day of the teaching work week.

At the school district, an efficient secretary showed them into the superintendent's office. He was sitting at his desk and didn't get up when they entered. He gave a questioning look, and Margaret spoke. "We came to sign the contracts you offered us when we were here with Howard Morris."

The superintendent gave a shrug of his shoulders. "Oh, we hired somebody else instead."

And that was that. Rendered speechless by his curt arrogance, with no explanation, no apology, just that shrug, Margaret saw his done deal was clearly their undone one. She sensed that Clara was as furious as she was, but there was little either could do to change the situation, although they could think plenty. Feeling the anger and adrenaline rush through her body and seeing Clara's clutched jaw and the flush on her face, it was all she could do not to tell him what a son-of-a-bitch he was. Something more than words crossed her mind, too, but she mustered all the self control she had and noticed Clara doing the same.

The man never knew how close to danger he was in that moment. And he couldn't know that there would be a time down the road when his broken promise would come back to haunt him.

It would happen a few years later when he would run for public office. Out on a handshaking campaign in the schools, he would encounter Clara. Offering his hand to shake, he would be refused with these words.

"I'm sorry, sir. I wouldn't vote for you if you were the last human being on earth. You're dishonest. You don't keep our word. You can't be trusted. When I get done with your reputation, nobody up here'll vote for you."

That candidate was not to win the election. We can't say for sure why, but maybe he didn't keep his word too many times and word of it got around, Clara likely playing a role here. Maybe his opponent was seen as a better fit for the job. But the former superintendent wouldn't be holding public office.

Yet, then in 1965, that broken promise created an unexpected challenge for the two soon-to-be ranchers. Despite this stumbling block, Margaret knew she and Clara would simply keep looking for jobs while they did the other things they had to do. They wouldn't let somebody like this jerk keep them down. So with the house in good-enough shape and minimal but sufficient work done on fences for the horses, they pointed their car east on Highway 50 to pack up for the final move.

And quite a move it was. Margaret knew that no other in her life could match this. Loading up at the old home place, she stood back long enough to take in the scene. There before her were their two dogs— Clara's Saint Bernard and her Weimaraner, a forty-two-foot semi-trailer filled with horses, five of which were mares with foals, then a stallion, and some other horses in between. Their wonderful trucker, Jim with Butcher's Truck Line, had built a special stall in the front of the semi for the stallion, then some places for single horses, the brood mares, and a compartment in the tail end for the foals. On this five-hundred-forty-mile trip, they planned one stop for the babies to nurse.

She looked at the pickup truck. It was full of boxes, suitcases, furniture, including a deep-freezer full of meat on which all kinds of possessions were stacked. Her old Chevy also overflowed with belongings they'd need for their new life. A big load to match the big change before them, and a giant step toward their dream.

Heading out early, Margaret drove her Chevy, the good ole car that had taken Clara and Frances around the Bay Area, transported them all from Oakland to Rago, and served her well during her two years of teaching here. Clara was in the pickup, and Jim commandeered the semi-trailer. Driving across the little creek and down the dirt road to the highway, she bade goodbye to life in Rago.

She'd appreciated her time here, the demanding but comfortable way of life on the farm and the kindness of Clara's family. She'd learned a lot about living close to the land, all of which she could now put to use on her own, on her and Clara's land.

She knew she would visit, but she was on her way to her new home. Looking in the mirror, she caught Clara's attention and waved, thinking that similar thoughts must be going through her friend's head.

They made good time on the two-hundred-thirty mile stretch to Syracuse, Kansas, near the state line. Then just outside town, under low grey skies, Margaret saw the roadblock. Her heart sank as she pulled to a stop, and then it sank some more. The officer who'd approached the car was telling her that an unusual weather pattern had caused heavy rainfall in Colorado, and in some eastern and southeastern parts of the state unprecedented rain. The South Platte Basin, Sand Creek, the Arkansas Basin were all flooding. It was a major flood. Stunned, for a moment she wondered why he was giving her a weather report, but then he said, "You can't go any farther west. You're gonna have to turn around and go back home."

By now, Margaret realized Clara had come up beside them, saw she'd heard enough of the unwelcomed message to know what was up, her mouth tight and hands clutched into fists. Tension emanated from her, and Margaret heard her words as if they were an echo of her own unspoken thoughts, "We can't go back! We have live animals, and we've gotta get them to Colorado. We're headed west of Pueblo."

She watched the patrolman's head pull back, a thoughtful look come into in his eyes, and she knew Clara's desperate words and tone had made an impression.

"Maybe if you go up to Limon from here, then get to Colorado Springs and back down to where you're headed, that might work."

Knowing Limon lay about a hundred-seventy miles northwest,

Margaret sighed. It wasn't exactly on their way. But what choice did they have?

In Limon they found more trouble. The flooding had made every route impassable. They would have to stay there until the floods subsided.

The stranded travelers looked for a motel and were glad to find one with vacancies. Bone-weary, as she knew Clara and Jim were, too, Margaret stood at the ready while Clara explained their plight to the motel owners, a wife and husband team. She admired, once again, how articulate Clara was regardless of circumstance as she noted the couple's sympathetic looks. Then her jaw dropped as she heard the response.

"You can park your pickup here and plug your freezer in. We just went out of the Appaloosa business, and we have a barn down on Sand Creek. Corrals, stud pen, mare and colt runs. Everything. Use what you need," the woman said.

"Miracle" was the only word that came mind. Margaret felt relief rush over her and saw it mirrored in Clara's eyes. With relief and good directions their companions, the caravan made its way to the barn. It truly was a perfect place, Margaret thought, as they unloaded the horses, finding good spots for each. They fed the horses and dogs and put their sleeping pallets in the barn's feedway.

Pulling together a quick, simple dinner of provisions they'd brought along, Margaret wondered of all the times in her life she'd been tired, if she'd ever been *this* tired. She couldn't wait to lie down on that inviting pallet. Then sleep overtook the weary traveler before she could ponder her question very long.

They spent two nights in Limon. On the third day, the caravan traveled the one hundred fifty miles to their dream ranch in the Wet Mountains of Colorado.

5

Not-Your-Nine-to-Five Job
1965 –

THEY NAMED IT SINGING ACRES RANCH, FOR THEIR DEEP LOVE OF singing and for the way the land sang to them. Being in its lush meadows and magnificent mountains, it was impossible not to hear its melodies. They thought Julie Andrews singing, "*The hills are alive, with the sound of music …* " captured their joy in it perfectly.

At various times they could hear its other inhabitants in the ongoing chorus. Birdsong of all kinds, chirping, twittering, gurgling, gabbling, rat-a-tatting, squirrels chattering, elk bugling, a fawn mewing to find its mother. The flapping of wings in an otherwise silent day, or the heart's trill when encountering a wildflower in brilliant bloom. They were completely enchanted.

As I am when I find myself back in its magical forests, inhaling evergreen scents, watching the leaves of tall, white-barked aspen quiver in the slightest breeze. It's a place of great beauty, nature in all her glory. I'm enchanted and also aware, as were Margaret and Clara, that nature's glory is also fierce. It's not a one-dimensional deal.

That nature's ongoing food chain of predators and prey includes foals, chickens and other ranch animals as likely targets didn't escape them. And if they didn't already know, they soon learned that winters at that altitude are harsh with deep snow, ice, wind, below zero temperatures. Spring is wet and muddy. Summers can bring drought, lightning and fire. And fall, well autumn brings gold to the hills, brilliant color that poet Robert Frost warned was nature's "hardest hue to hold."[1]

Such were the conditions in which they nurtured their animals,

---

1 Robert Frost. "Nothing Gold Can Stay," *Selected Poems of Robert Frost*. New York: Rinehart Editions, 1963, 138.

helped mares foal, cared for the newborns, improved their home, barn, fences, and found ways to earn a living so they could continue doing all this. They managed it through their seemingly unending reservoir of resourcefulness and, as we now say, working twenty-four/seven. And all along, they always found time and energy to help others, a tendency we'll hear more about later.

Four decades on, Clara, looked back on those times and said, "I don't know how we did it. I just always said we had strong backs and weak minds." Many of those who've known them would agree with the first part, but not a soul would concur with the second. They were strong, smart, determined and equipped with a bottomless well of hope, humor and, of course, love for that place. They had to be to accomplish what they did.

CONSUMED BY GETTING THEIR RANCH IN SHAPE, THE TWO NEW RANCH- ers also had to figure out how to earn the money to pay for it. Howard had been generous in his financial arrangements, but he wasn't giving the ranch away. They had payments to make, along with animals to feed, improvements and general maintenance to attend to.

Given the setback with the no-show Florence contracts, they contin- ued applying to school districts within driving distance and also looked for additional ways to bring in some income. Pretty much anything legal and ethical was on the table. When the opportunity to work with Quintan Engleman, balling and bagging nursery trees and getting into the Christmas tree and bough market came along, they signed on.

At the time, the money was in pine and fir, and Quintan knew where to find it. Sometimes for special orders he sent them the seventy or so miles north to Guffy or to the next big range over to dig particular trees. Clara, who'd grown up hauling wheat and knew how to drive a big truck, delivered the orders to Denver. She thought that was the easy part. The hard part was digging up the trees and getting them ready to move.

An eight-foot fir tree might not seem all that big, especially when you consider that it can grow to seventy-five feet or more. But Clara knew this size tree was almost three feet taller than she and Margaret.

It was heavy and its root system spread out plenty wide. Digging it up, usually in hard, rocky soil, and getting it ready to move was where the grueling work lay. Then the biggest challenge came in getting those spreading roots into a ball and securing the ball with burlap. And finally, loading the whole thing on a tall, deep truck. Even with the two of them, it was tricky and challenging. Given the number of trees they had to wrestle, it was taxing work, indeed. They did it well.

As for the bough part of the job, Clara watched Margaret put her extensive tree-climbing experience to good use, shinnying up trees to cut limbs and drop them down to her. Clara herself got darn good at breaking the limbs into appropriate lengths and wrapping them for market. She figured that together they cut and wrapped tons of Douglas fir boughs, much of it from their own land.

Their own land. It took a lot to tend to it. But the land gave back. They just needed to see its possibilities, listen to the melodies, heed its refrains. It was in doing so that another idea came.

Clara often commented to Margaret how on bright, blue-skied winter days, the snow-blanketed hill across from the house looked positively silver. Its gentle slopes beckoned, and although she wasn't a skier, she and Margaret knew others were. That silver hill could become a ski area.

A ski area, even a small one with only beginner slopes, would be a big project, and they knew they couldn't do it by themselves. They soon learned others were interested. Through a mutual acquaintance, they met Glen, who lived in Pueblo, and they started talking.

On one occasion Glen brought Joe along, a contact Glen thought might put up some financing. Clara liked Joe. She thought he was quite a character, colorful in his speech and kind of fast-talking. She could sense he'd taken a liking to her and Margaret. One day he turned up at the ranch without Glen and in his brand-new, top-of-the-line Impala Chevrolet. When he asked to take them to lunch in Canon City, they thought, why not. Off they went and, at Joe's insistence, with Clara at the wheel of that beautiful new Chevy.

At the family-owned Italian restaurant they settled in at their table and ordered lunch. So far the conversation had been light and casual, then Clara noticed Joe's face get a little more serious. She thought he had something on his mind and wasn't completely surprised when he said, "Don't youse women get involved with Glen. He's all talk, no work, and you'll end up losing everything."

Clara watched Margaret's eyes focus in on Joe. He went on, "You want a ski area, I'll help you. Don't get involved with him."

Then Margaret glanced at her and nodded ever so slightly, and Clara knew that Joe's words had had the intended impact. As they had with Clara. They both figured Joe knew what he was talking about. They also figured that, although they really liked Joe, keeping a little distance from him might not be a bad thing.

Heading back to the ranch, Joe asked Clara, "How's you like the car?"

Her answer came readily. "It's great!"

"Then it's yours."

"No, no, no. I don't want your car. I couldn't afford to buy tires for it."

"I'll buy your tires."

"I couldn't let you do that. But it's nice of you to think of it."

Clara knew he wanted to help them, but for months they continued to refuse all kinds of gifts because they just didn't want to get involved. She also knew he had money and that he gambled because he'd tell them about it.

"Well, I won eight hundred dollars last night," he'd say.

"That's a lot of money!" she'd reply.

"Yeah, but I lost a thousand the night before."

And so it went. He never bragged about his winnings.

They didn't know if the rumors of his association with the Bohemian Mafia, a term sometimes used for those with Czechoslovakian heritage in the organized crime scene,[2] were true. Nor did they know if he really was a gun runner. But Clara did know her gut told her to keep some

---

2 The actual Bohemian Mafia operated in Prague and parts of Czechoslovakia circa 1916 as a group working to create an independent Czech state, using some of the Sicilian intrigue, without the violence. See *Eastern Europe: Introduction to the People, Land and Culture*, by Lucien Ellington, Richard Frucht, ed. ABC-CLIO, Inc. Santa Barbara, CA: 2005, 230-231.

distance and not be beholden. In my experience, Clara's gut responses were pretty much always on target.

Yet, they liked him and enjoyed talking with him. To Clara he was somewhat like her older brother, Gale. Both were World War II vets. Joe'd been a Marine Corps paratrooper, Gale had been in the infantry. She thought Joe kind of acted like Gale. Easy-going, genuinely kind, fun, with a steel core.

Over time, Clara watched Joe realize that he was dealing with two very self-sufficient women. Finally, with some reluctance, he admitted it. "Okay, you don't need my help, but if you ever get in trouble, I can fix any judge in Pueblo."

Clara hoped with all her might that they would never get in that kind of trouble. She couldn't know that Joe Valley, whose given name was Joseph John Valentich, would appear before many judges and was a known associate of the Smalldone organized crime family. That upon his death almost fifty years later in July of 2014 at the age of ninety, *The Pueblo Chieftain* would publish a story about him, which included this observation from a police officer and long-time acquaintance.

> [Joe Valley] associated with a certain element in the community whose status was somewhat questionable in what they did and didn't do. He was very active but also very careful. He was like the 'Teflon Don.' We could never get anything to stick.[3]

The lively friendship with Joe continued for several years, long after the ski area became a reality. He'd stop by the ranch, want to take them to lunch or just visit. But they never had to ask him for help with the ski enterprise. Aid came in another form, soon after they'd taken Joe's advice and dropped the idea with Glen.

Florence Hoza, a new friend who lived in a nearby cabin, led them to it. Clara had been visiting Florence and in conversation told her about their idea. Their chat turned out to be a lucky one. Florence's son Kenneth had long been interested in that hill for a beginner's ski area. Clara was amazed and also grateful that a solution lay right under their noses and

---

3 Jon Pompia, "Underworld figure dies in Denver," *The Pueblo Chieftain*, July 30, 2014.

that taking action on it was so easy. She and Margaret formed an official partnership with Kenneth and they were on their way with the project.

They called it Silver Hills Ski area. From the outset there were nay-sayers. Some of the locals did not want it built. "It'll bring in all kinds of trash."

"There will be too much traffic."

"Where will people park?"

"It would just be terrible," they said.

Clara thought people often fear things they don't know anything about. She knew this from working with kids, and she knew it from observing human nature in general. But to appease those with concerns, the partners promised, "We'll do it. We'll build the ski area. But if it causes problems, we'll close it down."

They built it. It didn't cause problems, and it wasn't terrible at all. Turned out just the opposite. Clara knew Margaret and Kenneth were as pleased as she was that countless local kids, many who wouldn't have had the opportunity otherwise, learned to ski there. Numerous families spent delightful days together on that perfect beginner's slope, and on the other slopes when additional tows appeared.

Newspapers in Pueblo and Colorado Springs featured articles on Silver Hills. People drove from Pueblo, they came from Westcliffe and other places in Custer, Fremont, Pueblo and El Paso counties. As many as three hundred skiers on a very full day, around a hundred on an average day. And they had fun.

Along with staff for the certified professional ski school and a sea-sonal lift operator, the partners hired four teenagers to work every day the area was open, which was on weekends, primarily from January through March, when the snow was at its best. The teenagers chose between working half a day and skiing free the other half, with lunch thrown in, or working all day and getting paid for it, lunch included. Whatever they chose, they would remember it always.

In 1976, ten years after Silver Hills opened, Conquistador Ski Area in Westcliffe started up. Clara wasn't enthusiastic at all when the initiators came to her and Margaret trying to get them involved. "No thanks," they both said, with some emphasis.

"But why not? You certainly know the business now, and this will be a much larger operation."

"You're not putting that ski area in a good spot. It's just not a good idea to put it in where there's no protection for those slopes. They're wind targets."

They did put it in that spot. And indeed, many days when the wind blew, howling around the slopes and whipping up the powder, Conquistador's tows couldn't operate, sending countless skiers fourteen miles down the valley to Silver Hills.

Four decades later, Clara admitted her surprise that they operated Silver Hills for twenty years. At some point along the line, Kenneth sold his share to Clara and Margaret, and the two kept on going. That is, until climatic changes helped them realize they didn't want to do it anymore. All along, Clara had had mixed feelings about it. Sure, it helped them pay the bills, but it was work-intensive, and it had to operate during the school year. With the ranch, the tree and bough business, and the ski area there was a lot to pay attention to. And the insurance was a major headache. She was more than relieved when they realized they could and should end it.

You'd think the two women would've had enough platters spinning, since by January of 1966, Margaret had a teaching job in Pueblo at Bessemer Elementary School. Then only a few months later, in March, Clara was teaching in Pueblo County's Pleasant View Junior High School. Yes, it was junior high school, but it was a job, and she held out hope that she could work her way to high school level for which she was better prepared.

Their drive to work was forty miles, and they knew they needed economical, reliable transportation. A Volkswagen Superbug fit the bill, but they needed a way to pay said bill. They knew a bank loan wouldn't be possible, and they didn't have the cash to buy it outright. But help came from a surprising and mysterious source.

They'd met Sister Betty through Margaret's long-time friend Shirley Ward, from Oakland. Sister Betty lived in Shiprock, New Mexico, and came up to help them out during her weekends off from her nurse-midwife position on the reservation. Clara knew Margaret appreciated Sister Betty's help as much as she did, and especially liked that the nun often brought other nuns, midwives and nurses along to assist, too. They'd do all kinds of chores from milking cows, churning butter, hauling firewood, to feeding chickens and more.

On a visit to the ranch, Sister Betty heard about the new dilemma. She asked how much they needed. Clara said, "Twenty-one hundred dollars."

Without a moment's hesitation, Sister Betty said, "I know where I can get it."

Before long, they got a letter from a woman named Miss Flick, who wrote, "I hear you girls need a loan to buy a car. It'll be two percent interest and you pay it back however you can."

Clara replied immediately, thanking her and telling her the terms they could manage. "We'll send you fifty dollars a month, plus two percent interest each month."

And each month they faithfully sent off a check. When the balance was down around five hundred dollars, they received a neat note in Miss Flick's elderly handwriting saying, "With your last payment, I consider this note paid in full."

ANOTHER NUN AND ANOTHER PLATTER TO SPIN CAME THEIR WAY during the eventful time they were building the ski lodge in 1966. This nun came along looking for horses and help for a riding program. Clara soon learned that Sister Estelle was associated with a Benedictine order of nuns based in Chicago. The order had established mission schools and programs in Colorado, one of which was Saint Scholastica Academy, a boarding school in nearby Canon City, as well as a local summer camp program. The latter was what Sister Estelle wanted help with.

She'd heard about Clara and Margaret and wondered if they had some gentle horses on which they could give a few of the girls who attended their summer camp riding lessons. Several kids had been injured at the camp where they'd been riding, and the Sister was searching for a way to get them over their fears brought on by the accidents. The search had taken her to Singing Acres Ranch, to Clara and Margaret.

It didn't take the two ranchers long to talk it over. Thinking out loud, Clara began listing the advantages. "With our experience at the Flying G, this is right up our alley. The numbers are small and this camp would be coming to us."

Margaret chimed in. "We have the horses and space. It'll be in the summer when school's out, and when we're not messing around with trees, boughs, or the ski area."

To Sister Estelle they said, "Yes, we have the horses, and yes, we can help the kids get over their fears and learn to ride. We'll do it."

Clara knew their horses were bomb proof. Gentle as they came. She'd made sure of that, taking them through their paces in all kinds of situations so they overcame any fear or nervousness. The girls came one or two days a week, and she and Margaret worked slowly and carefully with them. They knew they first had to talk a frightened kid into getting back on a horse. It took some time and effort. Both knew better than to rush any part of the essential healing before getting on with the learning.

Clara watched the girls' steady progress in learning to trust the horses, then begin to feel comfortable just being on horseback, and then pick up the reins of riding. It was working, as she knew it would, and she was happy for those girls. It was working so well, in fact, that Sister Estelle came back with another request. "Would you consider doing our whole summer riding program?"

Clara felt that what they'd earned from their limited work was good, and the offer for more was even better. It would make their land payment, that big mortgage payment that fell in the summer. She and Margaret were in perfect accord on it.

"Yes!" they said. In unison. And once again, they were off.

A seamless complement to their horse-breeding program, Clara thought. She well knew that when you have a color breed like Appaloosa, you're going to get a lot of plain-colored colts, and although they're equally good horses, they're not as marketable as the loud-colored ones. People were drawn to the horses with blankets across their back ends, or leopard spots all over. That's the coloring generally associated with Apps. It was clear to Clara that training the plain-colored colts to work in the camp string made good sense.

She loved Appaloosas for the way they looked, but she also treasured their natural tendencies toward tractability and versatility. Apps wanted to please and they were good at a wide range of roles from stock horses to excelling in a variety of equestrian activities. And a whole lot of them appeared in movies, especially westerns. In their horse business, she figured they could either sell the loud-colored ones off the bat, or train them for gymkhana events and rodeos so they'd bring more money when they were sold. And the plain-colored ones really were ideal for the camp kids learning to ride.

Usually, St. Scholastica contracted for ten horses, which Clara thought was just about right. She used the ten for teaching the girls horsemanship and also for trail rides. Sister Estellee would let her know in advance if they needed more. And even better, St. Scholastica provided the insurance, an expense Clara knew they wouldn't have been able to cover.

As was the case at the Flying G, their riding program aimed primarily to teach the girls to ride, respect horses and be safe. Safety was prime, and by emphasizing that with the girls, they saw very few accidents, and no serious ones. By the end of camp, they'd have the girls playing games on horseback and riding drills. Clara put her experience in Saddle Club to use, teaching the girls how to do the Grand March, a precision riding drill, and pretty much everything else associated with riding. And watching Margaret work with the girls, she recognized just how far her friend had come from that first day at the Flying G. Not only could she saddle a horse practically blindfolded, she was great at teaching the kids what they needed and wanted to learn. Which was generally everything.

The program was so successful that ultimately the camp really did come to them, to Clara's delight. St. Scholastica leased forty acres on the southeast corner of their property, put up a crafts building, and later a larger building for a kitchen and dining room. A mobile unit housed staff and served as the infirmary. The girls slept in big, floored tents. Beginning sometime in June and running to the end of August, half the girls would be at the Singing Acres horse camp, named Camp San Benito, while the other half were in Canon City doing other kinds of camp activities. Then halfway through the summer, they'd switch places.

It amused Clara that most of the girls were from the Chicago area, which made sense, she thought, since that was where the order was based. She got a kick out of how much they loved being in the mountains, how new everything was to them, and how eager and curious they were. And later on, the kids were from even farther away, cream-of-the-crop kids from places like Mexico City, whose wealthy parents wanted to send them to camp to learn English. The irony to Clara was that she and Margaret learned a lot more Spanish than the girls learned English.

With the riding program and camp in full swing, they were able to make the ranch payment with no problem. The steady income from teaching and the other seasonal income from the ski area and tree business made it possible for them to keep the animals fed and to continue making repairs and improvements on the house and the ranch. Within five years, they realized they had come a long way, were putting in the hours to make things happen, and they were elated by every bit of it.

Sometimes they had to call in others, as they did late one night, when they discovered a mare down and in distress in the meadow. Clara knew the situation was beyond her, that she needed expertise different from her own. At the time, there were no local veterinary clinics and so they resorted to the phone book. There they found Dr. Shiner in Canon City, thirty-five miles away. Clara felt relieved and grateful that he would come all the way to the ranch at that hour. She felt even more so when he was able to help the mare.

By the time he'd seen to his patient, it was getting on to midnight, and all three were exhausted. Clara was glad Margaret extended her usual hospitality and invited the doctor in for a cup of coffee. She was surprised, however, that he accepted, because in her experience, vets didn't normally say yes to such invitations. But she welcomed the opportunity to talk more with the doctor about the mare and the follow-up treatment she'd be giving.

Sitting around the old oak table in the middle of the night, sipping strong, hot coffee after the intense experience, Clara felt the complete absence of barriers among them as they chatted like old friends. Much of the talk centered on horses, which Clara was always happy to discuss. But then she got a surprise from Dr. Shiner when he looked from her to Margaret and back, and asked, "Why on earth would two women buy a ranch in this high country and raise horses?"

Exploding with laughter, they gave Dr. Shiner the straightforward answer he deserved; one they'd given many times before. "Because we wanted to!"

Clara would feel the warm camaraderie of that evening with the good doctor for many years. She and Margaret developed great respect for him, thought he was a wonderful veterinarian and friend, and she never ceased appreciating all she learned from him.

I wasn't surprised to hear about Dr. Shiner's curiosity about these two ranchers. But where he was kind and genuinely curious, others were less so. There were those who wondered what those two women were doing raising horses in that rough country and were betting they wouldn't make it even a few weeks, a few months, and especially not a few years.

And there were the rare ones who tried to make it even harder. One guy tried to bilk them on hay prices. Another they bought bulk gasoline from charged them more per gallon than other customers. Clara got wind of this from one of the kids at school and acted on the information right away. Going directly to the guy, she said, "We found out what you're doing with the gasoline prices. We won't be buying from you anymore."

No grudge, no retaliation, just no business.

Clara guessed that people just didn't understand how, much less why, they could spin all these platters at once. People didn't realize that the two ranchers felt excited and exhilarated all the time, in no small part because people were constantly saying to them, "You can't do that!"

And they would say, "Why not?" and go on doing it.

What people also didn't realize was what tough stock Clara came from. Her grandfather, Rudolph, had been a hard worker—a carpenter, farmer, manager, and good father to a large family, and her father, Arnold, had followed suit. Margaret's father and her friend Mac had contributed to her strong foundation for overcoming hardships. The determination of both women was solid and endless. As were their kindheartedness and optimism.

Clara's take was that for the most part, people were supportive. The Falkenburgs at the hardware store extended them credit for building supplies, letting them make payments that better fit their constrained finances. Jennings Market also ensured that their payments were manageable.

"Even so," Clara later mused, "a lot of men wanted to hide and watch, and a lot of women were rooting for us. That part was funny."

I TRY TO PUT MYSELF IN THEIR PLACE, THERE IN THE MID- AND LATE sixties, having the time of their lives while working their butts off, challenging stereotypes without caring whether they did or not, breeding, training, selling beautiful horses, riding them all over the mountains, mountains then unfettered by fences and developments. They were living the life they wanted, in a place they loved.

At the same time, they were creating opportunities for kids with the riding program, and kids and families with the ski area. They were changing things for themselves, and by who they were and what they were doing, they were changing things for others, not the least of which was an understanding of what women are capable of. All of this on their ranch, their land, in the mountains and meadows that sang to them then, and would for the rest of their lives.

PART II
Voices of Singing Acres

Margaret, Clara, visiting at home, circa 2002. Courtesy Clara.

6

A Community of Friends

FRIENDSHIP ECHOES THROUGHOUT THE MOUNTAINS, MEADOWS, AND forests of Singing Acres Ranch. I hear it and feel it each time I'm there. The sound of laughter as puns fly back and forth in the kitchen, the murmur of voices in deep conversation, or the peaceful silence that welcomes anyone, anytime. Sometimes it's through the barking of dogs when a truck, car, or four-wheeler pulls into the yard, which is often. And I can almost hear the wagging of dog tails when alerting turns to welcoming, whether friend or stranger.

"Compassion, vitality, generosity, and comic understanding ... characterize the best friendships." This is a slight rephrasing of Ronald Sharp's portrayal of Eudora Welty's fiction in their co-edited book on friendship.[1] What a perfect description of Margaret and Clara's friendship, and of that which radiates from them out to others.

Another fitting essay in that anthology stands out, helping me think about friendship from yet another angle. This one from Aristotle who more than twenty-four hundred years ago wrote about three kinds of friendship. The three he describes are all reciprocal, but they're distinguished by motive. One motive is usefulness, and in this case, affection may or may not enter into the picture. If it does, it's likely affection for the good each person gets from the other.

Then there are friendships driven primarily by pleasure. Aristotle said, "We love witty people not for what they are, but for the pleasure they give us."[2] He thinks most often young people's friendships are

---

1 Eudora Welty and Ronald A. Sharp, eds. *The Norton Book of Friendship*. New York: W.W. Norton & Co.,1991, 30-31.
2 "From Nichomachean Ethics," Aristotle, *The Norton Book of Friendship*, 67-70.

based on pleasure—fun, adventure, novelty. He calls these first two motives, usefulness and pleasure, "incidental" kinds of friendship because they center on what one gets from another, not on interest in the person for who she is.

And then we come to what Aristotle considers the perfect form of friendship, and that is between people "who are alike in excellence or virtue." Most importantly to me, he says, "Those who wish for their friends' good for their friends' sake are friends in the truest sense"[3] because they truly care about the person.

I appreciate Aristotle's distinctions, while knowing there are many other ways of viewing this so taken-for-granted topic. Whether at the Flying G, in their schools and classrooms, in their churches, or at their ranch, within their own generation or across generations and ethnic or racial groups, Margaret and Clara cultivated friendship in all its facets, through difficult times, shared pleasure and their caring about others as individuals. This is why so many of their friendships were life-long and continued to deepen over time.

And this is why the heartbeat of community echoes here, too, for the ranch is a hub around which friends, family, neighbors, acquaintances and stray passers-by converge. It's a rare day when fewer than six or seven people don't drop by to ask about a horse, pick up a dozen eggs, bring a pie, seek advice on any range of issues from carpentry to a child having trouble in school. Each is welcomed with sincere warmth, even when the two ranchers would like nothing more than a few quiet moments to themselves. Instead, they listen to and share stories; they learn from others and offer what they know. They build trust. They build connections. By simply being who they are, they create community.

In her book *Full Circles, Overlapping Lives*, Mary Catherine Bateson, sage daughter of anthropologists and social scientists Margaret Meade and Gregory Bateson, writes about learning from every encounter we have. She says, "Wisdom comes not by accumulation of more and more experiences but through discerning patterns in the deeper mystery of

---

3 Ibid

what is already there." Margaret and Clara didn't seek novelty. They sought depth, and they found it in their land and in the people around them. Bateson writes, "Wisdom, then, is born of the overlapping of lives, the resonance between stories."[4]

Overlapping lives, the resonance between stories. Wisdom. Clara and Margaret invited people into their lives. They cultivated friendships and circles of friendships. What better way to learn about them than by hearing stories from some of those friends, some of that community that formed around Singing Acres Ranch?

4 Mary Catherine Bateson. *Full Circles, Overlapping Lives.* New York: Random House, 2000, 172-173.

7

Who ARE Those Ladies?
1966 -

Melanie Camper was on the cusp of her eighth birthday, Margaret and Clara both nearing thirty, when their paths first crossed one June day in 1966. The brief and early encounter wouldn't provide any clues to the way their lives would intersect over the next four decades, nor the impact, in all its variety, they would have on each other. But to Melanie, that meeting was memorable, a modest but noteworthy prelude to what followed. Putting myself in Melanie's shoes, I can imagine how it, especially in concert with several others soon to follow, would make an impression on a lively, curious young girl. Here's how I think it unfolded.

Having just finished second grade, Melanie reveled in those early days of summer vacation. Summer meant she could do all her chores and still have time to ride her bike the two miles to town and up and down the smooth concrete sidewalks. That was so different from the gravel, rut and rock roads out by their ranch, which she willingly pedaled on. But the flat, flowing streets and sidewalks on which she could glide seemed like heaven.

She was glad her friend Connie could go that day. She and Connie always had fun together. Wheeling down Second Street, a street the locals, for some puzzling reason, called Dutch Row, she spied a couple of ladders on the sidewalk propped against the building. Two strangers were painting on the big storefront windows.

The girls stopped to watch. One person was painting while the other held the paint for her. The painter's brush moved surely and quickly across the big panes and, as if by magic, cartoon-like images began to appear—bucking horses and bulls snorting out smoke, their dancing hooves whipping up clouds of dust. It seemed the figures were actually moving. She realized they were advertisements for the upcoming Westcliffe Stampede and she thought they were great.

Melanie loved the Stampede, the popular local rodeo. Her grandfather and dad had been among its founders way back in 1947, long before she was born. She knew that it had started as a community event that local ranchers, her grandfather and dad among them, hosted. It'd been so popular that it'd grown into a two-day event and part of the Custer County fair.[1] What she didn't and couldn't know was that this was the painter's first time to paint the windows for the Stampede, and that she would continue to do so every June for the next four decades.

Melanie and Connie gawked as the enthralling images unfolded before their very eyes. At the same time, those eyes took in the two unknown women, both dressed in jeans, boots, and cowboy hats. Melanie was impressed by all of it, the paintings and the way the strangers were dressed. Those clothes were right up her alley.

The paint-holder smiled at them and asked, "What are you girls doing?"

"Just watching you paint," the wide-eyed Melanie said.

The woman smiled again and nodded as she leaned down to pick up another container of paint while the painter went right on working. Melanie and Connie couldn't wait to get themselves and their bikes far enough away so they could talk about how cool they thought that whole scene was.

July came, Melanie celebrated her eighth birthday, and rodeo time drew near. While the grown-ups were working to get the fairgrounds ready for the big event, the kids were playing all around the place. Melanie and her friend Idelle had their horses with them that day, and soon they found themselves over on the racetrack. Melanie really liked that racetrack, its grooves so clearly marked by all those hooves that had pounded over it for years.

---

1 See *http://www.americancowboy.com/travel/rodeo/great-rodeo-circuits* for more background and information.

Under its spell, the girls started running their horses around and around, excited by the running, therefore running more and faster, until the horses' chests began heaving and their mouths frothing. But they kept going, thrilled by the speed and daring of it. They took the horses around yet another time, and as they passed the grandstand, a woman stepped out, grabbed one of the horse's reins and pulled it to a stop. The other horse slowed and stopped, too.

Astonished, Melanie stared at the woman, saw the firm set of her jaw and serious expression on her face. She spoke. "Girls, get down off those horses. That is enough. You give those horses a break."

Melanie was speechless, but the woman wasn't. "When you start seeing this," she continued, pointing to the froth as the girls dismounted, "you know the horses need a break. You don't run them till you see all this sweat and foam."

Bug-eyed with fright, Melanie choked out, "Yes, ma'am."

The woman turned to walk back over where others were painting the stands, and Melanie realized it was one of the women she and Connie had seen doing a different kind of painting downtown a few weeks ago.

She turned to Idelle, who was as wide-eyed Melanie thought she herself was, and asked, "Who ARE those ladies?"

ALL TOO SOON, THE STAMPEDE WAS OVER, THE DAYS OF AUGUST HAD flown by, and Melanie was back in school. She was in third grade. Walking into her classroom that bright September morning, Melanie got a big surprise. Standing by the door to welcome the students stood the lady who'd stopped her horse, the lady who had been holding the paint for the other stranger, the lady who was her third grade teacher. That lady was Miss Clara Reida.

Later in the day when she went to art class, Melanie got her second surprise. The art teacher was the painter with Miss Reida downtown in Westcliffe that June day. And although she taught second grade, Miss Margaret Locarnini also taught art. Now she knew who those ladies were. She couldn't believe it.

But before long, Melanie realized it was okay with Miss Reida, better than okay, really. Miss Reida didn't frighten her a bit. Sure, she meant business and she didn't put up with any horseplay. There was time for fun, as well as time for work, with a good bit of attention paid to practical matters, to using your common sense.

Around Miss Locarnini, however, she felt intimidated and scared. Much later down the road, after many experiences with Miss Locarnini, Melanie would acknowledge that she wasn't mean, but she was often gruff. She'd know that to a kid "gruff" can translate to "mean"—and it's hard for a kid to get past that early impression.

Although Miss Reida had been the one to scold her about running the horse too much, and although Melanie never forgot it, she responded to the teacher's warm and genuine concern for her students. Being in her classroom for most of the day, Melanie could see how this teacher wanted to reach her students and wanted them to understand. She liked the way Miss Reida would get them involved in their own learning, mainly because she taught them things they didn't pick up anywhere else, like proper telephone etiquette, how to introduce people correctly, how to write a letter from start to finish, address an envelope, and a whole lot more. And she taught it all in ways third graders could understand.

Melanie would have occasion to laugh about this etiquette forty-some years later when that same teacher would pick up her own phone, answering with a "Yeah?" And even more so another time when she'd answer in a tiny voice, "This is Peggy," imitating a popular television commercial. It would always make her laugh.

Of all the impressions third grade left on Melanie, she thought losing her appetite for tapioca pudding might be the strongest. Tapioca pudding ranked high in her choice of desserts, and her mom made a great one. Melanie loved it, she really loved it. And she loved the pudding served in the cafeteria. She loved it, that is, until one fateful day when the cafeteria's pudding preparation went awry. Melanie wondered if maybe it was with the measurements. There was too much or not enough of something in that pudding.

A boy sitting at the lunch table with Melanie and some others pointed it out. "Look at this!" he shrieked.

He began pulling the pudding up and out with his spoon. It stretched and stretched, then popped back down. He did it again and then exclaimed, "It looks like a bunch of big boogers."

That did it for Melanie. She had a weak stomach anyway, and the kid's demonstration and comments were just too much. She couldn't even try the pudding, couldn't lift the spoon to her mouth. Leaving the table with her plate, she went to the trashcan to scrape it off but was stopped by the day's lunchroom monitor. Miss Locarnini. Miss Locarnini didn't like to see kids waste food. She asked, "So how come you're not eating that?"

"I don't care for it. It's gross," Melanie replied.

"Well, there are a lot of things in life you're not going to care for. Kids are starving all over the world, and you're not going to waste food," Miss Locarnini told her.

Melanie longed to say, "Put it in an envelope and send it to them." But she longed to be outside at recess a lot more. Scooping the pudding onto her spoon, she plugged her nose and stuffed the gross stuff in her mouth. She swallowed it and handed in her tray.

"Good job," Miss Locarnini said. Melanie nodded, stepped outside the door and threw up all over the floor. She didn't know she had eaten enough to make that much of a mess, but the proof was before her. And she'd thrown it all up in front of her classmates. She was horrified.

It got worse. Miss Locarnini came out of the cafeteria and saw the scene. Melanie couldn't know that the teacher was surprised and her "face-up-to-what-you-don't-like" response, drilled into her by her stepfather, had kicked into high gear. That she wanted Melanie and other students to be able to move beyond obstacles of any kind. All Melanie knew was that she looked at Melanie and the mess on the floor and said, "Go to the janitor's room. Get the mop and bucket, and get that cleaned up."

By then, Melanie was vomiting even more, and she was crying. Her sixth-grader sister, Cindy, came around the corner and saw her.

"What happened?" Cindy asked.

Between sobs and hiccups Melanie choked out a reply, "Miss Locarnini made me eat that gross pudding, and it made me throw up. Now she says I have to clean it up."

Cindy walked straight over to the nearby pay phone, dropped a coin in the slot, and dialed their home number. "Mom, you'd better get up here, cos' I'm fixing to kick Margaret Locarnini's ass!"

"No, Cindy, you can't do that." From across the hall, Melanie heard her mom's voice coming through the receiver gripped in Cindy's white-knuckled fist.

Mrs. Camper didn't go to the school, and Cindy didn't kick Margaret Locarnini's ass. But for quite some time, Melanie would have trouble remembering much about Margaret Locarnini. And she certainly blocked that event from memory for a very long time. But forty-one years later, she found it all came rushing back.

The memory would happen in the fall of 2007, not long after Miss Locarnini, Margaret to her by then, would be diagnosed with advanced-stage pancreatic cancer. Too weak to feed herself, Margaret would allow Melanie to help her. Melanie, sitting by the sick woman's side, spoon-fed her a food that was easy to swallow and digest—tapioca pudding.

Later that day she called Cindy. "You're never going to guess what I did today."

"What?"

"I fed Margaret tapioca pudding."

Her sister's laughter would bubble up, not from a place of vengeance nor as a reaction to the awful situation, but from a deep sense of appreciation for humanity, for who we are in all our dimensions, and for irony. Melanie, who by then had gained a profound appreciation for Margaret's sense of humor, would feel a circle of healing and would describe it as "God's way of knowing there was mending that needed to go on, else you'd have this little-kid-association all your life about a teacher you felt so intimidated by." Melanie hadn't held on to the association all those years, but she would have always felt some uncertainty about Margaret. That uncertainty would vanish on that day, and only caring and appreciation would remain.

MELANIE BECAME AWARE SOMETIME IN THE NEXT FEW YEARS THAT MISS Locarnini left Custer County School District to teach in larger Canon City, although she couldn't have said just when that change happened. She'd see her when she'd go skiing at Silver Hills, the wonderland that made it possible for her and so many others like her to learn to ski. What a magical place it was to this grade-schooler.

Melanie ran around with her older brother, Jim, and sister, Cindy, both of whom got in on the deal of working at Silver Hills on weekends, either for a paycheck or half-day's work for a half-day skiing. It was clear to her that the nearness of the ski area and the deal the two ranchers/teachers offered introduced, as she would later say, "a million kids up here to skiing who would never have had the opportunity otherwise." Herself included.

A few of her friends went to Monarch Pass Ski Area, about an hour and a half northwest of Westcliffe. When they talked about the chair lift, she was completely mystified. How could someone get on a chair with skis attached to their feet? At Silver Hills with its rope tows, she could ski, which she loved, and she didn't have to worry about a baffling chair lift, long drives or overwhelming expense.

ALONG ABOUT SIXTH GRADE, SHE FINALLY TALKED THE OWNERS INTO letting her work the concession stand. By this time, though she was still intimidated by Miss Locarnini, she came to think of her as pretty fun. It seemed the teacher could separate herself from school and the classroom. She could be someone just renting skis to eager skiers, and she seemed to enjoy doing it, teasing everyone, even Melanie.

"You'd better not tear these up," Miss Locarnini would say, titling her head and raising her eyebrows.

Returning the playfulness as she grabbed the skis and headed outside, Melanie would yell, "I won't!"

Melanie liked the lighter side of Miss Locarnini.

THEN SHE WAS IN SEVENTH GRADE, FINALLY HAVING MOVED UP TO JUnior high. On the first day, Melanie walked into English class to find that her teacher was Miss Reida. And as it turned out, Miss Reida would be her English teacher all through the rest of junior high and high school.

Melanie loved how Miss Reida would tell horse stories in class, most likely when she wanted to illustrate some point. But the kids could get her going on those stories, so Melanie thought, to avoid homework assignments. But Melanie never wanted the period to end, she was that enthralled by what Miss Reida was saying, particularly the detail she would so often go into.

Melanie had horses, and she could ride. She knew how to work with them. She could certainly tell you whether a horse was a bay, a chestnut, an appaloosa or a paint. But Miss Reida could talk about their breeder bloodlines or what characteristics you could expect if you bred this horse with that one. It all had to do with a kind of equine genetic logic, and she loved it. She was also savvy to the fact that Miss Reida was on to the students' motives and that she encouraged the idea they were getting away with something when she hadn't planned an assignment in the first place. Miss Reida was pretty coy.

She was also amazingly understanding. When Melanie's grandfather had pancreatic cancer and felt overwhelmed by the disease, pain and hopelessness caused him to take his life. Devastated by his death and the manner of it, she didn't want attention called to herself. Somehow Miss Reida understood this. As Melanie later described it, "She was very good about sneaking over next to you when no one was paying attention and saying, 'Boy, I'm really sorry. If you ever need to talk about it, or it gets rough and you need to be alone, all you have to do is look at me and raise your hand as if you have to go to the bathroom.'"

Melanie appreciated that Miss Reida knew kids have a lot of pride, that she respected kids even when someone had screwed up and was in trouble. That's why they respected her. She wasn't like those adults who'd say, "It's just teenage stuff." Miss Reida understood that it was real to you, no matter what your age was.

It impressed Melanie that Miss Reida took on as much at school as she did in the rest of her life. She was always sponsoring clubs, producing plays—comedy, drama, it didn't matter. They were consistently great. Miss Reida, along with another teacher, Mr. Thornton, who taught math, in Melanie's view did a wonderful job. They worked well together, and once, when one of the kids Miss Reida and Miss Locarnini were concerned about and were trying to help needed a good example in the how-a-man-treats-his-wife-and-daughters-with-esteem department, Miss Reida asked Mr. Thornton for help. Mr. Thornton took the kid in, and that made all the difference in the world in terms of that young person's idea of relationships and his understanding of people treating each other respectfully.

Yes, respect was a big theme when it came to Miss Reida. Kids respected that this teacher would set boundaries, draw the line, physically if necessary. It made an impression on students, Melanie included, when this lady, dressed so pretty for class, had to take a teenage boy to the floor. And this, Melanie thought, could happen publicly only if no private alternative was available.

I can just see it.

In the hallway outside the classroom, one boy corners another, threatening him. Miss Reida, dressed in a subtly patterned skirt that falls a little below the knee, white blouse and low heels, comes upon the scene and tells him, "Dean, you'd better go into the classroom now and take your seat."

Dean refuses. He says, "Not until this wimp apologizes to me."

"You need to go now."

"I'm not moving," Dean growls.

Whereupon Miss Reida strongly guides Dean against the wall, looks straight into his eyes, and through clenched teeth says, "Now!"

Dean moves quickly into the room and to his desk. Miss Reida follows and stands beside him. "Don't let me catch you hounding Phil or anyone else again." Dean doesn't, there's no need.

Most commonly, Melanie observed, when a kid was in trouble and she had to persuade him to go to the office, she'd wait till he stepped out of the classroom to grab him by the ear or nape of the neck before marching him down the hallway.

Inside the classroom or out, Melanie looked up to Miss Reida. Miss Locarnini, too, now that they'd had some better experiences together at Silver Hills. But she didn't see Miss Locarnini much, except during ski season weekends. She felt drawn to Silver Hills, and she also felt a powerful pull to Singing Acres Ranch. That was because of the horses. Horses. Miss Reida's knowledge of horses and Melanie's deep interest in them was a definite bond. When Melanie'd drive by SAR and see trail rides setting out, she'd think. "Aw, I wish I could work for them."

On the family ranch, Melanie worked with horses, or rather, she worked on horseback. Herding cattle, fixing fences, putting up hay, and everything else ranch-related she did. It was never-ending hard work. There was no foaling or raising foals because her parents bought horses ready to work. And there were never any recreational trail rides. At some point later on Melanie would realize that some of the people on those trail rides would've given anything to be out chasing cows and doing the kinds of cowgirl stuff she did day in and day out. But at the time, that thought never entered her mind.

Very likely inspired by Margaret and Clara, Melanie and Marla, her best high school friend, had a dream of getting a ranch together and raising horses. It never came to pass because, as Melanie later described it, "Life happens and you go on and do your thing and don't come back to your dream."

In Melanie's mind there were two or three good girlfriends that she could've gone the ranching route with, if they had matched up with other of life's demands at the right time. Timing was essential, as was respecting what the other person brought to the partnership, something she clearly saw at Singing Acres. She could see that Miss Locarnini respected Miss Reida for her knowledge and her love of animals and the country life. And later on she saw how Miss Reida admired and supported Miss Locarnini's interests, expanding as she did into every aspect of construction—carpentry to masonry—cooking, art, and more.

MANY OF US HAD A TEACHER WHO HAD A CLEAR IMPACT ON HOW WE saw ourselves and how we aimed our lives. Someone who recognized a worthy individual in us, who taught us to see beyond our current circumstances, to be curious, to have hope and be flexible. For me, that teacher was Miss Martin.

I was in seventh grade in a little one-room mountain school, grades one through eight. Miss Martin invited me to Sunday afternoon tea, which was so special I clearly remember, these fifty-eight years later, the tea in a pot, cookies on a platter, and Miss Martin sitting gracefully and attentively on the sofa as I perched on a chair across the tea table from her.

Miss Martin invited all ten of her students, grades one through eight, to recognize the many ways in which learning takes place by taking us on impromptu field trips to identify lichen, trees, and rocks. Reading the classics to all of us, teaching us to play chess and organizing hotly-contested spelling bees and other games. Miss Martin is why I became an educator, why I spent thirty-plus years in and around schools trying to help pry the system away from uninspired, pressurized teaching practices.

Miss Reida was Melanie's Miss Martin. And to some extent, Miss Locarnini was, too. Melanie described it best. "By these ladies showing up and being who they were, they were saying, see, you can be a horse wrangler, you can do all these things, and still be a teacher. They were setting standards for kids. For me, that meant you're an okay person even if you'd rather be out there wrestling a bale or getting dirty 'cause that's what it takes to have these beautiful horses. It's okay for you to do that and still be a professional, a teacher, and a good role model. They were the first ones here telling women, just by what they were doing, you can be whatever you want to be and pushing them along. It doesn't mean you can't be a good mom or keep a good home, but if you want, you can do other things, too."

That's who those ladies were.

8

Straight from the Heart
mid 1960s –

H E LOOKED AS THOUGH HE'D STEPPED RIGHT OUT OF A LARRY McMurtry novel as he walked toward the corral where I stood that sun-filled July afternoon. Tall, fit, handsome, blondish hair tousled by the breeze, moustache, cowboy boots, a Western belt buckle, and all. Yes, he could've doubled as a younger version of Gus in *Lonesome Dove*.

"Danny?"

"Yes ma'am," he replied, a broad smile spreading across his face.

"Carol," I said, as we both reached out to shake hands, his grip firm and friendly.

"I remember," he assured me.

We were at Singing Acres Ranch, and I had been exercising Z-Dog and Nacho, Clara's big, lively canines. Clara was off visiting a terminally ill friend near Westcliffe, a younger woman who'd lived with her and Margaret back when she was a teenager and going through a particularly rough time. They were close, and Clara had planned to stay with Ginnie for as long as she could that day.

Danny Cartmill had come to see Clara and was planning to watch over the ranch until Clara got back from Ginnie's. He'd arrived earlier than we'd thought he would, making good time on his more than five hundred-mile drive up from Medford, Oklahoma. I was glad we'd over-lapped because I wanted to talk to him in person, to ask if I could inter-view him about Margaret and Clara. Danny and I had met numerous times, but there were long patches in between, so a face-to-face meeting seemed a good way to raise the interview question.

"Yes, ma'am, you certainly can," he replied, offering his phone num-ber and address.

Danny's easy manner reminded me of something Clara had said about him, first commenting that she'd known him "since he was a grasshopper." She'd said, "There's something so pleasant about him, he restores my faith in humanity."

Even though I didn't know him all that well, I felt I knew exactly what she meant.

Several weeks passed before I called for that interview. Danny was about to leave for Texas, where his job as a hands-on problem solver who could repair almost anything for a big oil company was taking him. His expert training in firefighting, so valued in that business, along with other skills, made him in high demand all over the country. We agreed on a time to talk, and then that time had come.

WHAT STRUCK ME MOST IN OUR CONVERSATION WAS DANNY'S UTTER devotion to Margaret and Clara. From the time he first met them in the late 1960s when he was six or seven years old, a grasshopper, he loved them, that love growing stronger over the years. He considered them both his other moms. He felt especially close to Margaret, possibly because of their shared love of hunting and fishing, which they did so much of together. After Margaret died in 2007, he built his own memorial for her, several lines of which read, "Mentor, Friend, Artist, Hunting Partner, Fisherman, Teacher, Rancher, Religious World Traveler." The last line says, "Proudly I call her Mom," and he signed it "Danny Cartmill, Jr., Son."

With Clara's blessing, he placed the memorial back in the far reaches of Singing Acres Ranch, in the spot that was his and Margaret's favorite. It's under a big ponderosa on the edge of a meadow filled with wildflowers in the spring and summer and framed by mountain tops all around.

Clara took me up there one day on her four-wheeler, up hills, across gullies, past the old original homestead, and through the forest. Their favorite place feels remote in the best kind of way, and it is. Large stands of aspen border the meadow, ponderosas dot it here and there, as do high alpine rock outcroppings. It's so quiet back there you can hear the birds' wings flapping as they fly far overhead.

I took in the large metal plaque Danny had crafted and engraved and wondered how anyone could not be moved by the unaffected emotion it held. A horseshoe cross stands next to it, made by Danny's son, Daniel Cartmill III, now a computer specialist with a big oil firm. The two tributes warmed my heart as I thought how simply and straightforwardly they spoke to Danny and Margaret's friendship. Their placement in that beautiful remote spot seemed perfect. Altogether they offer a poignant reflection of a deep and lasting bond across three generations.

A neighboring rancher who happened to be up in those far reaches of the ranch one day saw it and for days after exclaimed to people all around Westcliffe that he didn't know Margaret had a son. Clara heard about it, smiled to herself, and never said a word.

If you've ever had a favorite spot, you'll understand how Danny and Margaret treasured theirs. They'd sit for long spells under that ponderosa, supposedly waiting and watching for game. Sometimes, I guess, they actually did watch, sometimes I know they didn't. They hunted together almost every year for thirty years, so they had ample opportunity to conduct those trips however they saw fit.

It was Joe and Donna Davis, longtime friends of Clara's family back in Kansas, who were the link for Danny and his family to Singing Acres Ranch. His parents, Marge and Dan, Danny and his two sisters were on a double-family trip out west with Joe and Donna when Joe suggested they stop by to see the ranch and introduce the Cartmills to Clara and Margaret. The introduction led to a lasting friendship. The Cartmills, Clara and Margaret would stay in touch, write often, visit each other, and come to care deeply about what happened in each other's lives.

When Danny was old enough, around 1975, he and Margaret started hunting together. This was the first of their annual trips continuing until 2006. Danny learned a lot about hunting from Margaret. He loved to hunt, and Margaret was a great hunting partner and mentor.

Once, though, when they were out, Margaret shot an elk over on the far side of a big hill. Even to Danny it seemed like a lot of work to get that elk out. After that, all they'd have to say to the other was, "How far over the hill is it?" and they'd both bust out laughing. The elk and the slog it took them to get it back were just more cement for an already solid friendship.

This experience and others he found hilarious, but what touched him about Margaret's hunting was how she'd give so much of the meat to families who really needed it. And she'd do it in a way, he said, that wouldn't draw attention to herself. Sometimes she'd leave packets of meat in someone's car where she thought they'd find it right away. When she knew one of her students needed other food or clothing that the family couldn't afford, she'd leave those things in their car, too. In Danny's estimation, Margaret was about the most kind-hearted and generous person he'd ever met. He hardly noticed her tough outer shell because he knew very well what a softie she was inside.

Margaret and Clara both inspired him because they were always doing something for someone. He couldn't get over the fact that they could be let down or hurt so many times and still not turn their backs on someone in need. But he noticed that they were particularly interested in helping people who wanted to help themselves, who strove to be self-reliant but had just hit some obstacle that was making that difficult. Like some of the kids they took in till they got over a rough spot, or a single mom who wanted to get some training so she could better support her family. As with Ginnie and others in difficulty, and there were lots of them over the years.

In a different way, they'd taken Danny in, too, right into their hearts. He thought they felt protective of him, wanting only the best for him. Although Margaret, in particular, didn't always trust him to make the right decision. This was the case with his marriage to Cindy, whom Margaret didn't know well. So she took it upon herself to test Cindy to see if she was really the right sort for him.

It happened soon after Danny and Cindy were married, when they were at the ranch during hunting season. Cindy, exhausted from the long trip up from Oklahoma, was taking a nap on the big recliner in the front room. At the same time, Margaret was butchering an elk and put aside the heart; she had something special in mind. She slipped into the house and gently laid the elk heart on the sleeping Cindy's leg, then tiptoed to the kitchen to wait and watch.

Cindy snoozed on. One of the cats spotted the tempting treat, jumped up on the recliner and started chewing on the heart, which in turn woke Cindy. She looked down at the cat and the elk heart and without missing a beat, flipped the heart off her leg onto the floor. And went right back to sleep.

That did it for Margaret. She didn't get the scream she'd expected, didn't get much of a reaction at all. No further testing was needed. Cindy was in.

All along, Danny took the pranks in stride, and he loved their sense of humor. They could laugh at themselves, and they could set up situations so he could laugh at himself, too. Like when he was a kid, Margaret would command Scarlet, their Chesapeake Bay retriever, to drag him off the couch. Scarlet would grab his clothing and take him down. Danny told me he didn't stand a chance, so he just gave in and wrestled the dog, enjoying the tussle.

Sometimes they'd all be out on a trail ride, and Clara would ride by and steal the bridle off the horse he was riding. Danny didn't consider himself a country boy who knew all about horses and might know what to do if any old horse lost its bridle. He didn't think of himself as a city boy, either, like Margaret sometimes teasingly called him. And although he'd ridden horses, this was different. He'd be on that horse wandering around in the woods for a bit before the horse would fall back in its place in line. After a time or two, he learned more about how to use his body to guide the horse. And he realized that the horses Clara trained were pretty much bombproof and that hundreds of kids had ridden them without incident. Still, he was the one on that horse wandering through the trees, and at first he felt bewildered. Then, as a result of those wanderings and learning to guide a horse with his body, his confidence grew.

Danny admired what Margaret and Clara had accomplished with the ranch, the horse business, the riding camps, the ski area. There they were, two teachers, doing all this, living in a pioneer home heated only by wood, giving to others and, obviously, enjoying it all. Teasing and pranks included.

Although both of them would jump in to do anything, Danny could see a natural division of duties the two had worked out. Margaret took care of the building and repairs. Clara did everything for the horses. Margaret would go out and build the barn. Clara would take care of what lived inside, horses, cats, whatever needed care.

Margaret was the cook, Clara did the dishes. Danny ate many a memorable meal at the ranch. Margaret didn't throw food away and she didn't make small batches of anything, so there were usually hefty amounts of leftovers. He noticed that the first day, whatever the dish, it would be really good. The next meal, it would still be good, but a little spicier. By the third day, the food would be so spicy hot from the chiles Margaret added that Danny, who wasn't accustomed to much heat, couldn't eat it.

But he enjoyed the big write-up the *Fremont County Sun/Trader Food Section*[1] did on Margaret. In it the reporter asked "How do you cook necks and bones, and why would anyone want to?"

"If you know how to cook them, you'll never throw them away again." Margaret countered, and continued with instructions for her neck and rib specialty.

Had they interviewed him, Danny would have raved about the specialty, along with the recipes Margaret gave for spaghetti sauce, wild rabbit, venison stew and bar-b-que sauce. First-day, and maybe second-day, servings, that is.

Of the many articles about the unusual ranchers, one that made Danny smile was in the *Colorado Spring Sun*[2]. Explaining why she hated to shoot elk, Margaret said, "They are so beautiful. I do it for the meat, not the sport. Trophy hunt? I've never found a good recipe for antlers."

---

1 "Conversations in the Kitchen: Marge Locarnini/Teacher, hunter, 'fiercely independent,'" *Fremont County Sun/Trader Food Section*, October 3, 1979, 1-2.
2 "Independent Rancher Enjoys Rugged Life," *Colorado Springs Sun*, December 2, 1979, Section E, 1-2.

Danny knew Clara didn't like to hunt. In his eyes, Clara was more of a people person. He knew she didn't like crowds but he thought she dealt with people a lot better than Margaret. She wasn't quite so impatient or ready to take offense; rather she would listen and want to hear what a person had to say.

As for Margaret, well, it was clear to him that Margaret knew exactly what she wanted and didn't need anyone else to approve it. She could build anything, could make anything from bookshelves to barns, and she could do it all on her own if she wanted to. Danny could see that her rough exterior, that manner that led people to think her gruff, hid a soft-hearted person, a cupcake.

Years later, in May of 2007, when Danny was forty-six, he felt an unusual pain, and it wouldn't go away. Cindy, a medical technician, said, "It's Sunday, there's no one at the lab, so let's go check this out."

When she saw the result of the test she'd done, she said, "You're coming to the hospital tomorrow to see the doctor."

But the next day he went to work, rather than to the hospital. Cindy called him. "Are you coming over here, or am I sending an ambulance after you?"

He went, and they found pancreatic cancer. Fortunately for Danny, thanks to Cindy's expertise and an early diagnosis, he got the saving surgery right away. The subsequent treatments were excruciating and debilitating, and they went on for months. But determined person he was and is, Danny stayed the course. And he credits his wife with saving his life.

I was on a visit to the ranch soon after Margaret and Clara got the news about his cancer. They were both heartsick and looked to me as though they'd both been kicked in the gut. Worse, they felt helpless, because there was nothing they could do for the boy grown into a fine man, whom they loved so much. For Margaret, it was the return of her worst nightmare—cancer in someone so close. First there'd been her dad. Then her sister. Friends along the way, and then Danny, whom she thought of as a son.

When Danny and I talked, I realized that it must have been frightening to Margaret for another reason. She'd also been having a lot of unusual pain, pain she'd been denying even to herself. Her way of coping with it was to have an extra drink or two. After a while, even that didn't seem to help. Toward summer's end, she finally saw a doctor. The news was what she'd feared, and because she'd avoided having the problem looked at for so long, the pancreatic cancer was not only aggressive, it was advanced. Her nightmare was back, in spades.

What a terrible irony that the two friends who'd shared so much in their love of hunting and fishing were sharing this terrifying disease. It was strange comfort, however, that they could talk with each other about it. They visited by phone, but Danny wanted to see Margaret in person, despite his schedule of treatments and their after-effects. He went to the ranch as often as his situation allowed, though it wasn't as often as he would've liked. But the trip he made to the ranch in October, between radiation and chemotherapy, was memorable.

Despite the fact that neither he nor Margaret had the strength and stamina needed for hunting, they could do something else they loved. They could go fishing, and that was Margaret's favorite thing to do. Her favorite fishing hole sat over on the Peterson ranch. They headed to it.

That property had long ago passed into the hands of longtime friends Pat and Tom Schulze. Pat once told me how it amused her that when Margaret went to fish there, she'd park her car where no one could see it from the house. Pat figured she needed time to air her brain, so she made sure no one disturbed her privacy. On this day, Danny and Margaret got to air their brains together.

Danny was fond of that fishing hole, too. He had always relished Margaret's joy in fishing, and he did so even more that day. He figured she knew pretty much anything there was to know about angling, and the thrill she got from catching a fish absolutely delighted him. A fine day and a chance to be together doing what they loved, and at that place—it seemed perfect to Danny.

Although he couldn't hunt, Danny was glad to hear that a few days later, neighbor and friend Jimmy Sewell took Margaret hunting. She was weak and alarmingly frail, but Jimmy drove her up to a place where they could watch for game. When they spotted their deer, he handed Margaret down out of the truck, then helped her lift the rifle and sight in. She fired, hitting her last target, her final game. The next day, October 29, 2007, Margaret died.

When you're expecting bad news and the phone rings, your heart may seem to stop for a moment. It's almost as if the ring is different, as if it's some sort of alarm or warning. Perhaps that's what Danny felt when he heard the phone that day when Clara called to tell him that Margaret had died. He knew it was coming but still, it took his breath away. And when he could breathe again, the only thing he could think to do was to send up a prayer for his friend, his hunting partner, his fishing buddy, his other mom.

Margaret herself was gone, but the memories were not. And Clara and Singing Acres Ranch still held a special place in Danny's heart. The following years saw him hunting at the ranch and cutting firewood for Clara, a task of necessity, satisfaction, and love.

Once when he was hard at it, he noticed a black bear watching him for a while. Then it ambled away. When he went back to the house, he saw the screen on the kitchen window had been broken. As he walked in through the front door, he heard noises toward the back. Running toward the sound, he arrived just in time to see the bear scramble out the back door.

He guessed the bruin had smelled food and crawled in through the kitchen window. The evidence was clear that the big, furry critter had eaten the food, drunk all the water, opened all the cabinets, and left scat in all the bedrooms.

The next morning Danny looked out the kitchen window, and there was the bear, looking right back at him. He called the game warden, who came out and set a trap. About two hours later the bear fell for the trap and was taken off to a new home.

The incident with the bear reminded Danny of the range of

experiences he'd had at the ranch and how they kept on coming, a reality he welcomed. He'd learned so much from Margaret and Clara at this magical place, and he counted his blessings for it. A high regard for the land and how to take care of it, the importance of feeding and taking care of the animals, the domestic ones, that is, before attending to yourself, and the need to reach out and help others in need.

Danny is one of the most earnest people I know. He's soft spoken, thoughtful, kind. His response when I asked if I could interview him for this book, "Yes, ma'm, you certainly can," spoke volumes. Clara's observation about the effect his battle with cancer has had on him adds more. "He was a good guy before, but after all he's been through, he's wonderful. He appreciates the value of every minute."

In the mix is the fact that Danny never expected to live to meet his grandson, whom he worships. He also didn't expect to lose Margaret so soon. Somehow he's managed to find peace with it all. Maybe his time at Singing Acres Ranch has helped, along with being with his grandson and other loved ones. I agree with Clara. He is wonderful, and I also sense that he pays attention to and appreciates life in every aspect. When he speaks, it seems straight from his heart. He's a man both Margaret and Clara have been proud to call Son.

Margaret (right) and Louise Locarnini, circa 1939. Courtesy Clara.

Clara, circa 1941. Courtesy Clara.

Left: Clara with father, Arnold, and sister, Virginia. Right: with brother Gale, both circa 1938. Courtesy Clara.

Sisters: Virginia (back), Zelda (middle), Clara, circa 1939. Courtesy Clara.

Margaret, birthday pony ride, circa 1941.
Courtesy Margaret (Aussie) Locarnini.

Margaret (standing), first signs of teaching prowess, circa 1942.
Courtesy Margaret (Aussie) Locarnini.

Left: Margaret, circa 1958. Right: Clara, 1959. Both courtesy Clara.

Singing Acres Ranch house, 1965. Courtesy Mildred Halle.

Singing Acres Ranch house, mid-1990s. Courtesy Mildred Halle.

Singing Acres Ranch house, early 2000s. Courtesy Clara.

Margaret the hunter, circa 1975. Courtesy Clara.

Preparing to set up camp, Sister Josepha and group. Courtesy Clara.

Margaret (standing), Clara (right), riding camp, circa 1967.
Courtesy Clara.

A slice of Silver Hills Ski Area, circa 1972. Courtesy Clara.

Brand new Snowbird, May 10, 1992. Author photo.

Clara with a mom and foal, circa 2005. Courtesy Clara.

Margaret, circa 2006. Courtesy Linda Gulinson.

Margaret at her favorite fishing hole, 2006. Courtesy Clara.

Danny's memorial to Margaret and horseshoe cross by his son,
Daniel Cartmill II, 2014. Author photo.

Clara, Elmer Knight, and David Chrislip at Stillpoint, 2000. Author photo.

Clara at home, 2010. Author photo.

Last ride, Melanie Camper Fall and Clara, 2014. Courtesy Bridgette Reida.

Margaret's art in action, Harrison Elementary School bulletin board, circa 1990. Courtesy Clara.

One of Margaret and Clara's Christmas cards, by Margaret.

Another of Margaret and Clara's Christmas cards, by Margaret.

Grown-up Snowbird. Photo by Linda Gulinson.

POEMS BY CLARA

(1969)
Still strings
On a sleeping guitar ...
Low tires
On a waiting old car ...
Model planes
Poised in the air ...
Empty rooms
Whispering softly blare ...
He is gone.

(undated)
Little colt with wide startled eyes
Seeing for the first time
The width and breadth of skies.

Are you afraid?
You needn't be, you know,
Of plans well laid
By God.

Seek your mother now.
Seek her warmth
And she will show you how
To live.

9

Haven
1968 –

IMAGINE THIS: YOU'RE A HAPPY NINE-YEAR-OLD. A BIG PART OF YOUR happiness is being with your father, whom you love and who loves you. He's a good man, your father. He calls you Sport, takes you fishing, and builds model railroads with you.

Then, seemingly out of the blue, your mother divorces your father. She says you can never see him again. Next, your mother marries your father's stepfather, a cruel, abusive old man whom you had called Granddad but now are being forced to call Dad.

This new "dad" abuses you both physically and mentally, just as he did your real dad, as well as your dad's brother and sister. Your mother not only condones the abuse dished out to you but participates in every form of it mentally, while refusing to acknowledge the physical. You live this way for years on a ranch miles away from the remote mountain town where you were moved shortly after your mother married your new dad.

You have an older sister and younger brother living with you in this nightmare, although you slowly become alienated from each other, just as your mother and new father must have intended. You then become a rebel, although as a frail, skinny kid, your rebellion was laughable at best and often met with a good belting or bullwhipping.

Then when you're a high school senior and big enough to defend yourself, the accumulation of years of abuse comes to an end. Your step-father threatens you one time too many and you respond, meaning it, "If you touch me again, I'll kill you."

Some forty-six years later, Mike Haga described how he'd lived in this hell for seven years, until he could no longer endure it. He told me that although his mother had never intervened before, she did when the threat came from him and toward the stepfather. This time she called Sheriff Stan DePriest, and finally that hellish existence ended.

Now imagine the relief Mike described when Sheriff Stan arrived soon after the call, immediately telling the mother to pack some clothes for Mike. When she'd done that, the irony of her call became apparent.

"I'm taking Mike to a safe house," he told her.

Stunned, she said, "He should be going to jail for threatening his stepfather. That's why I called, so he'd go to jail, not to some safe house."

Stan told Mike to take the paper bag full of clothes his mother had packed and get in the car. Mike was quick to oblige. As they drove to their destination, the sheriff told Mike something that astonished him. He said, "Everyone in Westcliffe and the Wet Mountain Valley has known for some time what's been going on there. Unfortunately, nobody could do anything until someone called me in. Now your mother has made that call, although for a different reason, and you don't have to suffer the abuse anymore."

Mike didn't know what Stan had in mind for him, possibly a foster home, which would likely require navigating legal channels. But whatever it was, he knew it could only be an improvement over what his circumstances had been. When Stan headed to a ranch east of Westcliffe, Mike had no way of knowing how much of an improvement it would turn out to be.

The two ranchers who lived there had helped kids from troubled homes before. These ranchers were also teachers, and they knew young people well. Mike was surprised that one of them was his English teacher, Miss Reida. And the other, Miss Locarnini, taught elementary school. What they offered, a secure, welcoming environment, was exactly what Mike needed. He also craved a way to be useful, and the ranch held infinite opportunities for that. He could contribute in many ways and be part of the ranch family.

I can't fully imagine Mike's terror, the long years of cruelty so intentionally directed at him, nor his suppressed fury at his situation. How could I? I've never experienced anything close to it. And because I can't know or even imagine that, perhaps I can't know his immense relief, his sense of hope in being set down in a place of kindness and support. But I know that place of kindness and support, and I know it must have been a balm to his soul, as it has been to many others.

AS A SKINNY, INTROVERTED KID OF SEVENTEEN WHO CHERISHED HIS saving situation, Mike was afraid to do anything that might get him in trouble with his new family. He realized that at times both Clara and Margaret, as he soon came to call them, were frustrated by his reluctance to assert himself in any way. But he also saw and valued their patience with him, and slowly he began to relax, realizing the world wouldn't end if he did make a mistake.

As he emerged from his shell, his love for Margaret and Clara, whom he would ever after refer to as "the girls," grew exponentially. For the first time since losing his father, Mike began to experience what family signified. To him it meant love, acceptance, reliance, trust, and the desire to be the best he could be for his very special family members.

Later Mike would credit Clara and Margaret not only with saving his life, but for instilling within him a sense of self-worth, a desire to go to college and make something of himself. From the moment he arrived at Singing Acres Ranch, he felt safe and cared for. And he soon felt surprised by how much fun life could be.

Being at the ranch was different in every way from everything Mike had ever experienced. It truly was a whole new life. And even though each of them worked hard to keep the livestock fed, the house heated and the ranch running, while teaching or going to school, in Mike's eyes, they had ways of making it entertaining and enjoyable. The three of them worked in concert, in a way that complemented each other's efforts, and the laughing, joking, teasing only made it better.

The ranch house, made of logs, was more than a hundred years old. It had electricity and running water, but heating came from potbellied stoves, a fireplace and wood cook-stove. Keeping the wood supply re-plenished and the fireplace and stove going were Mike's responsibility, and he had to learn how to do it properly. Mastering the correct way to light the cook-stove offered a memorable lesson; in an early attempt, Mike dumped too much kerosene on the wood. When he touched the match to ignite the fuel, a small explosion lifted several cast iron pieces a few inches off the cooktop and singed his eyebrows completely off.

Once it was clear Mike was okay, he, Margaret and Clara laughed themselves silly. But he realized his own laughter was partly from relief, and no doubt so was Margaret's and Clara's. That was one close call, and funnier in retrospect.

Mike found that even the discomforts of the old house had their rewards. The upstairs bedroom that was his wasn't completely sealed, and sometimes a little snow would blow in from around the window frame. But the room, cold though it may have been, even a little snowy at times, was his sanctuary, his haven. He didn't have to worry about someone barging in at any hour to yell at or hit him. It was his own private space, and he loved it, including the old iron bed piled high with blankets, just right to burrow under. And he loved Bash, the huge, friendly St. Bernard, who latched on to Mike and shared his bed.

Mike and Bash had their games, running around the house, then inside through the kitchen and toward the living room. Mike would stop, but Bash's brakes didn't work so well. With his heavy, close to two-hundred-pound body going full speed, he once hit the couch and broke the back of it. Mike agonized about Margaret's and Clara's reaction. He was afraid they'd lose their tempers at him for his recklessness and destructive behavior. And when they didn't, it proved another lesson for him in kindness and acceptance.

Margaret's wizardry with cooking impressed him. He thought the meals she cooked were always beyond delicious, on to downright incredible. She could make the old stove hum and the pots and pans sing to her as she made the best meals Mike said he'd ever eaten.

The three of them worked well together, bringing their individual skills and willingness to tackle chores and everyday tasks into a kind of harmony. And it was a good opportunity for Mike to try some things he hadn't had the chance to do in his previous life. One was to go duck hunting, which he began to do with Margaret. Mike knew little about hunting or guns, but Margaret loved to go hunting on the Arkansas River with Smokey, her dark gray-black Weimaraner, and so on several occasions, Mike went along, too.

The three of them would cram into the sky-blue VW Beetle and set off down Hardscrabble Canyon road, memorable rides to Mike, every one of them. The road was steep with endless curves and switchbacks, and Mike would try not to think about lack of guardrails or shoulders to keep a vehicle from plunging off cliffs and falling hundreds of feet to Hardscrabble Creek. He tried not to focus on Margaret's driving, which he thought not the best on a good day and some days seemed to be downright reckless. Often scared half to death, Mike listened to her talk and laugh as he pressed on imaginary brakes.

Arriving at the river, with no small sense of relief for Mike, they'd set off for one of Margaret's favorite duck hunting blinds. Then came the waiting, the two hunters concealed in the blind, with Smokey lying in the grass between them. When ducks landed on the water, Smokey, without moving a hair or making a sound, would tense up, waiting for one of them to shoot a duck for him to swim out and retrieve. Neither hunter, to Mike's recollection, ever bagged a duck. By the end of the day, when a flock of the birds would land in the river nearby, a frustrated Smokey would dive in and attempt to get one himself.

One night Mike, Margaret and Clara went out spotlighting—nighttime rabbit hunting, using a bright spotlight, at which the animals would sometimes stare. Clara never hunted, Mike was only mildly interested, and Margaret was driving, so the hunting angle took a backseat to having a goofy time together outdoors.

Mike sat between Margaret and Clara as the truck bounced across hill and dale. Bracing a .22 rifle between his legs, he knew to keep the barrel pointing straight up. He guessed he must have had his finger on the trigger when they unexpectedly hit an enormous bump because the rifle went off, and the loud noise in the small, enclosed space deafened them. Three pairs of eyes looked upward to see the trajectory of the bullet, at once spying a perfect little round hole in the top of the truck. Their jaws hanging open, ears ringing, adrenalin flowing, they erupted into laughter that they couldn't seem to stop. Later, Mike repaired the hole with liquid steel. The hole may have been gone, but the memory was there to stay, and he'd laugh every time it came to mind.

Margaret fit the adventure companion role wholeheartedly, and to Mike, Clara filled the mother slot perfectly. After a long day of teaching, when dinner was done and the dishes washed, Clara would sit with him at the old oak round dinner table and help him with his studies. He'd come to Singing Acres Ranch with failing grades and the belief he was never going to amount to anything. He'd heard that repeatedly, for seven years, from the day his mother married his stepfather. But with Clara's patient nurturing and constant reinforcement that he *was* worthy and intelligent, Mike began to succeed and then excel. And he did so not only in English, but in his other studies, too. He knew it was Clara's belief in him, as well as his own hard work in applying his brainpower that accounted for the scholarship he won to Adams State College in Alamosa, Colorado.

Before his high school graduation, Mike worked at a local service station. With his first paycheck, he bought a thirty-gallon hot-water heater for the ranch, replacing the smaller one, and ever thereafter they all enjoyed ample hot water for their showers and dishwashing. Mike was thrilled to make this contribution.

Then came his graduation, and Margaret and Clara were there for the ceremony. He knew they wouldn't miss it for anything. It seemed to Mike that just about everybody else in town came out to wish him well, to give him cards filled with money to help with college. Moved and humbled, he'd had no idea so many people cared; so many people had been and still were rooting for him.

Off to college, Mike studied diligently during the academic year, then spent summers with his grandmother in Pueblo, painting her house inside and out, in lieu of rent. At the same time, he worked for the City of Pueblo Water Works. A busy life, yet he visited Margaret and Clara whenever he could. When his college graduation approached, they encouraged him to invite his mother and stepfather, telling him it was time to forgive his mother. Knowing her feelings about her and Margaret, Clara added, "If they do go, we'll step out of the picture."

Mike hadn't spoken to his mother for five years, but he did as Margaret and Clara suggested. He extended the invitation, and it was accepted. All too soon he had reason to feel that the acceptance came at a high price. Shortly after graduation, when at long last he'd reconnected with his brother and mother, he was dismayed to hear her ultimatum. "If you want to be a member of this family, then you can never see those people again."

"Those people." The people who had helped him when he was in trouble. The two people he'd come to love deeply. The friends who'd taught him to believe in himself and to know that he was capable of doing so much in life.

And now he was back with his own family, and things were different than when he was a kid, although not all things. In another way he was expected to give up an important part of himself, the bond with and connection to those he thought threatened his mother. But, in the end, Mike went along with her demand, although he did sneak an occasional visit to the ranch.

Deep inside, he knew he'd made the wrong choice, but he felt he'd made the choice and had to live with the regret that came with it. Around 1973 he went off to law school at Baylor University in Waco, Texas, losing touch with the girls. Years later, reflecting on that period, sorrow infusing his words, he said, "Why I ever made that decision, I don't know. The girls were my 'real' family and always will be."

But life went on, and it took him to Denver where he practiced law and began writing about the economy. Then in 1987 another event changed the course of his life, this one through a diagnosis that many people fear—cancer, and in his case testicular cancer. Mike feared it, too, and in his distress, he searched for reasons, wondering what went wrong to make this happen. Seeking possible sources, he thought of the trauma inflicted by his stepfather all those years ago. And although causes of this form of cancer remain unclear, in Mike's mind the abuse was the culprit.

The lengthy treatment and recovery periods were difficult for Mike, but successful. He pulled through, only to face a repeated diagnosis not long after. Again, the challenging treatment and recovery and again, excellent attention. As a silver lining on a very dark cloud, David Brothers, the physician's assistant who took care of him, became his life partner.

Around 1993, Mike invited David to accompany him on visits to his mother on her ranch near Westcliffe. Their route took them along highway 96, right by Singing Acres. David saw the old ranch house, a plume of smoke puffing out of the chimney, horses in the various corrals, chickens roaming free in the yard. He wondered how anyone could live up there, away from everything. Although the highway ran through the property, it seemed remote and rustic, with house, barn, corrals and mountains on one side and more corrals and big meadows and mountains on the other.

Mike, seeing his interest, began telling him about the ranch, about Clara and Margaret, and more details about how they'd helped him in really tough times. Sharing stories of those times with someone so close to him brought resolve. Mike said, "Next time we come down, we're going to stop by."

On their next trip down that way, they did stop. Mike was overjoyed to renew the bond. David's description, when I asked him about it twenty years later, said it well. "It was the biggest welcoming party that was ever given. It was like the prodigal son had returned home to Clara and Margaret."

And in terms of his own reception there, he told me, "We just hit it off, we did."

The connection never really broken, only suspended for a time, the bond with Mike was not only renewed, it was extended to David.

There seemed, however, an unfortunate pattern in Mike's life. As one bond was renewed another frayed, and in this case, once again, dramatically so. After Mike, David, and I talked about the reunion with Clara and Margaret, Mike described what happened next.

On their third visit to Mike's mother, she asked about their relationship. Mike told her they loved each other and were living together. A little later, as the dishes were going into the dishwasher, Mike smelled bleach.

"Why are you using bleach in the dishwasher?" he asked.

"I always do," she said, but went on to hint that there were diseases accompanying his lifestyle she now had to guard against.

Mike thought that now that his lifestyle and her biases were out in the open, she felt free to go further. He would never forget hearing her say that his partner wasn't welcome there. That she couldn't accept what Mike had confirmed about their living together. He could come back. David could not. In the face of another heartbreaking ultimatum, Mike decided he would not return either.

But the two did go back to Singing Acres Ranch. Every weekend they could get away saw them helping with chores, tearing out old corrals, "electrifying" the horse foaling structure, which was affectionately called "the condo," as well as buying and using a power wood splitter for the ranch.

The time with Margaret, Clara, and David appealed to Mike's need for harmony and sense of accord among those closest to him. Some of his best memories were of those evenings after the chores were done, after they'd all enjoyed one of Margaret's dinners, which Mike knew could have been elk, rabbit, pork, venison, beef, or something else Margaret simply described as road kill. Whatever it was, they enjoyed it, although David was nonplussed the time he found a chicken foot in the soup.

Sitting around the old stone fireplace, they'd talk about everything and nothing, and laugh at the spontaneous jokes and puns that seemed to sprout so naturally from their exchanges. Often Clara would talk about when Mike lived with them, how skinny and naïve he'd been when he came. How Margaret loved to tease him and how they laughed when

Mike finally realized he was being teased.

And before long, David and Mike were talking about the possibility of buying land close to the ranch and building their own house. Fortuitously, a one-hundred-sixty acre parcel behind Singing Acres was for sale, a parcel Clara and Margaret had wanted to buy to protect the area from possible development. The owner had refused to even talk with the two women about it, fearing they were a "couple," a claim they often had occasion to laugh at and off.

As the four friends talked about the possibility of buying that land, they became increasingly excited about the idea. The boys wanted to pay cash, but they knew it would be a stretch. The girls came up with a solution that seemed perfect all around. They would pay half the cost, David and Mike the other half. Mike made the call to the seller, and in his words, "they were off to the races."

They agreed on a price and set a date for closing within a matter of weeks. Mike and David were, almost literally, off to the races. They scrambled to raise their share, dashing around Denver to cash out bank and retirement accounts. Bankers looked at them askance, wanting to know why they needed so much cash and warning them of the dangers of having that much on hand. But they got what they needed and the deal went through.

By 1994 they'd bought the land, and the next year saw Mike and David having a little log cabin built on it. What began as a simple cabin became much more as they realized they'd need a big window in order to enjoy their stunning view of the Sangre de Cristo mountain range. Then, it seemed that the ceiling really ought to be vaulted, and maybe the fireplace should be larger, too. And so it went until they had, not a cabin, but a large, elegant home.

They lived in Denver during the construction but stayed with Margaret and Clara on weekends, continuing to help out with the ranch. Even after they'd moved into their new home, that simple log cabin that turned out to be so elegant, they continued helping. They'd feed horses, keep roads open, including those to Margaret's mother's and Aunt

Marge's homes up the road from Singing Acres, and helped the girls see to the family's needs. Marge and her husband, Darrell, had moved there in the mid-1970s, Dorothy and Mike followed in 1980.

In the fall they'd aid in slaughtering, dressing, and freezing Margaret and Clara's chickens. The ritual took place in the front yard where they'd fill a twenty-gallon barrel with water, build a fire under it and bring the water to a boil. Then when one of them had killed the chickens, they'd dip the bodies into the near-boiling water, then pull the feathers off. The final step involved eviscerating the birds, readying them to be frozen. They'd place each chicken in a plastic bag, usually a grocery bag, the fowl laid out horizontally. Mike and David would always remember those frozen chickens with their feet sticking straight out, almost a parody of rubber chickens. But they tasted mighty good when Margaret applied her cooking wizardry to them in the months ahead.

In the poultry department, David told me, he wouldn't soon forget the morning he slept in and Margaret slipped upstairs with a live chicken. Creeping into the bedroom, she carefully placed the hen under the covers beside him. Within seconds one of those two creatures literally flew out of the bed, and it wasn't the chicken. The hen was content to remain in a dark, warm place.

Wood gathering was hard work but it was also another source of delight. Mike appreciated the camaraderie that infused the demanding tasks—operating the chain saw to cut down trees, then cutting them into smaller pieces, throwing them on the truck, and taking them to the log splitter. The finale involved hauling and stacking all the wood. It amazed him that Clara always knew exactly how many cords they'd done. Taxing work, but a reason to be out in the fresh air, with dear friends and a gratifying result. Mike knew Margaret and Clara appreciated all that he and David did, and the boys willingly did all they could.

They both found Margaret's and Clara's openness and nonjudgmental attitudes impressive. Anybody could drop by and they'd welcome them into their home. One time when they were helping with some building, a young woman drove into the yard. Mike said, "If there was ever someone who looked like she was from outer space … I actually thought she was a vampire."

I asked for more description. "She had strangely streaked hair, multiple piercings, heavy, pronounced makeup, sharp teeth," David remembered.

Mike added, "But the girls just asked what she needed, which was a bathroom, and they offered her theirs. Then she was on her way." As he exhaled a deep breath, Mike noted, "No way would I have let someone who looked like that in my house."

Not that they thought the girls could easily be hoodwinked. Mike and David knew that both were naturally savvy, their skills and perceptions honed in the classroom, with parents, and in general. The boys knew the girls had had plenty of experience in their early years there to recognize when something was fishy. Both were good at that.

I asked how they thought Margaret's and Clara's natures differed. After a moment's reflection, Mike offered, "Clara seemed more content and steady, and Margaret more restless with that ongoing internal struggle people close to the two came to see sooner or later. Clara was naturally warm with people. Margaret held back a little more."

David chimed in, observing, "Margaret was a bit of a loner. She seemed to like doing things on her own, like going fishing. She'd take others along at times, but she liked going out by herself."

Intrigued by their thoughts, my mind cast back to others I'd talked with, their insights similar, only differing in phrasing. Mike summed it up. "Clara was just always so upbeat. Clara was steady, like the rudder, and Margaret was the current that could never [stay still]. Clara had to work with the rudder to keep the boat on course."

BEFORE MIKE AND DAVID MOVED INTO THEIR NEW HOME, DAVID HAD retired from nursing and had been devoting his time to running Economic Outlook Inc., a corporation the two had established to publish and promote Mike's books, newsletters and radio broadcasts. Mike's first book, *On the Brink: How to Survive the Coming Great Depression*

1993-2000[1], had done well, and he had a strong following. They'd believed that through the technology they'd enjoyed in Denver and expected be available in their new home, this work could be done anywhere. But they hadn't counted on the bedlam Mother Nature could wreak on a rugged, mountainous area that, despite Qwest Communication's assurance of high-speed data lines, lagged in technological infrastructure. But they were soon to learn.

The winter of 1997-98 brought particularly cold and harsh weather resulting in continual power outages that made their work all but impossible. The lines promised by Qwest Communications in 1994 still hadn't materialized, lines they sorely needed to operate their publishing business and for Mike to do his daily nationwide radio broadcasts.

Mirroring the weather, storm clouds developed in the friendship. Likely the clouds had been forming for a while, puffs of perceived expectations that had been accumulating bit by bit over time. Did the girls expect David and Mike to spend so much time every day helping out, plowing snow, feeding horses, splitting wood, or was that something Mike felt an obligation to do?

A light, chilly wind of assumptions began to penetrate the seemingly stout wall of friendship. Was Margaret's intention of building bookshelves in their new home something they wanted, or something Margaret wanted? Wondering about the forecast, Mike and David asked themselves, now that their simple cabin was their prized, luxurious home, did they want to share ownership of it? Thus, issues about the property title arose.

The title stood as Joint Tenants with Right of Survivorship. Essentially, this meant if any one of them died, legal right the land would pass to the surviving members on the deed. How would it feel, Mike and David asked themselves and each other, for one of them to die and the other to hold only one-third share? What if something happened to Margaret? To Clara? How would ownership play out?

Another factor came into play. In Mike's view Margaret's drinking

---

1 Published, Kansas City, MO: Acclaim Publishing Co., 1992.

had increased, or perhaps he was noticing more. He and David worried that Margaret's impulsive side coupled with a few drinks might result in a liability for them. They thought it over, talked it over repeatedly, added up the various factors, and then they proposed to the girls that they legally divide the land into two equal parts.

The reaction was not what the boys had hoped for. Mike thought Clara seemed hurt by the proposal, perhaps seeing it as a diminishing of the trust among them, a distancing of what had felt like family. And Margaret's tight-lipped curtness, her general behavior toward them, he thought held immense anger. He felt the girls didn't understand why dividing the land was so important, but the attorney side of him told him it was.

In retrospect, years later, he would come to understand that none of them was then able to see how myriad little things had led to the land-division proposal, an action that had crystallized the fact they'd been growing apart. The trust that had made it possible for them all to relax, open their hearts to each other, delight in each other's company, had corroded and left them looking, not at what had made them so close, but what had come to make them stand apart.

With blizzard conditions mounting in the friendship, along with the horrible winter of 1997, Mike and David became increasing frustrated with the situation. That one was, indeed, a winter for the record books. Several severe snowstorms shut down Highway 96, the main east-west highway, for days at a time. One storm brought five feet of snow overnight and additional snow soon after. The wind howled non-stop for weeks. Power lines came down, stopping operations at Acclaim Publishing. With the road closures, even driving to Pueblo for Mike to do his broadcasts was out of the picture. It was a miserable situation.

When in early 1998 David's father died, David and Mike went to Grand Junction, a town of about forty-two thousand people, west of the continental divide, for the funeral. There, in one of Colorado's sun belts, they found mild, sunny weather and stunning surroundings. They were smitten by the climate and the countryside, such a vivid contrast to snowy, rugged Custer County.

After a few more trips to Grand Junction, they decided to sell their new mountain home and move to a place more hospitable to their work and wellbeing. There, with the more moderate weather and ample access to the much-needed technology, they could conduct their business. In a new environment they could start again and create a fresh life for themselves.

I recall how upset Margaret and Clara were over the falling out with the boys, their dismay at how the friendship had fallen apart, the hurt and, yes, anger they felt from what had happened. Although at the time I didn't know all the myriad knotty details, I did feel that the boys' move seemed a good thing for everyone. Gone were the conditions for the frequent rub of misunderstandings and the distress it caused.

Hurt feelings take time to heal, if they do, but it can happen. Time for reflection, a chance to step back, a willingness to ask oneself what really went on—What role did I play in all that? What did I miss? Was there a pattern playing out in some way? How did the misunderstandings build so formidably, so swiftly? Did I contribute to it? How?

When I talked with Mike and David fifteen years later, time and distance had diminished anger, softened feelings and brought different, deeper understandings. After a long hiatus, they are again in touch with Clara. Indeed, it was she who suggested I talk with them. In their graceful older home in Grand Junction, surrounded by their gardens and vineyards, grateful that Clara wanted me to talk with them, they spoke of the misunderstanding, the anger, guilt, and remorse that accompanied that time.

But they also spoke, most eloquently, of love. Mike had always felt closer to Clara, and David to Margaret. But both talked about how much they loved both of the girls and what they meant to them. Mike spoke again of how the haven they'd offered him had changed the course of his life. For that he'll always be grateful.

As for that lovely mountain home near Singing Acres Ranch, some fifteen years later, Benny Reida, Clara's nephew, her late brother Gale's son, lives in it with his wife, Bridgette. They sold their home and land in Rago, Kansas, and came west to be part of the Singing Acres Ranch family. The hopes and dreams for which Mike and David built the house have changed ownership, but they surely live on in Benny and Bridgette. And now with old misunderstandings and disputes a distant memory, the connections between Clara and Mike and David have been renewed. The bonds of friendship and love, so integral to the Singing Acres community, remain a haven for all.

10

Overlapping Lives
1970 –

MARY CATHERINE BATESON'S APT REFLECTION ABOUT HOW LEARN-ing and wisdom grow out of overlapping lives, of the resonance of shared stories, persists in my mind. I think of her words and how, early on in Oakland, Margaret's life overlapped with Barbara Macgregor's, whom we know as Mac. Continuing long into the future, their friendship spawned more bonds and connections. And Margaret's and Clara's overlapped in a big way, making this story possible. Then Sister Betty came into the picture through a mutual acquaintance and eventually brought Sandy, whom you're about to meet, into it, too.

As trickles and streams from a spring run-off come together to create something larger, so did the many lives streaming in and around Singing Acres. They overlapped, converged, and sometimes diverged, often repeating parts of the sequence. That converging, diverging, and re-converging included Sandy.

OCTOBER, 1970, AND SANDY GREENE, A NATIVE UPSTATE NEW YORKER, was living on the Navajo Nation, in Shiprock, New Mexico. In New York she'd applied to work with Indian Health Services, not knowing exactly where she would be sent. And then there she was in Shiprock, living in an apartment on the big health compound that housed many of the personnel, including doctors and their families. She was a nurse in the medical surgical unit.

Sandy fell in love with the West. The vast cobalt sky, the soft hues of the immense desert, shadowed mountains off in the distance, the startling Shiprock formation, only ten miles away. Tse' Bit' ai', the Navajos called it. The Winged Rock. And it was sacred. All of the country felt sacred to Sandy, she treasured it. Those who inhabited it, as well. The miles and miles of dry desert and the warmth of the people filled her up in ways she'd not experienced before.

Folks she worked with, too. Especially Sister Betty Dougherty. Sister Betty had served as a nurse in World War II and subsequently became a Medical Mission nun. Sister Betty said her claim to fame was that her mother saw Al Capone's mother walking down the street. Sandy found that story quite funny, but she knew that Sister Betty had many claims to fame, not the least of which was, along with two other midwives, starting the first nurse-midwifery program in Indian Health Services. And it was right there in Shiprock. The other two, Lorraine and Sue, whom Sister Betty had met in Santa Fe after serving in India for some time, were still in Shiprock and were Sandy's friends, too.

Sandy thought there was nobody like Sister Betty, a bundle of energy topped with gray hair. The Navajos adored her; she commanded respect from everyone. Well-earned respect, in Sandy's opinion.

In one area, however, Sister Betty wasn't all that forthcoming. She'd leave town on her weekends off, never saying where she was going or what she was doing. Even more mysteriously, Sandy noticed the good Sister loading up her little Volkswagen with Navajo saddle blankets and other supplies. At the end of the weekend, she'd return with frozen chicken, deer meat "up the ying-yang" Sandy thought, along with eggs, and homemade butter. Notoriously generous, Sister Betty would share everything, except where she'd been or what she was doing. It really was an enigma, but Sandy figured when Sister Betty was ready to tell her, she would.

That day arrived. Sandy had the upcoming weekend off, as did Sister Betty. The two were beginning to discuss plans when Sister Betty, looking straight into Sandy's eyes, said, "Well, I've known you long enough now, and I'll trust you. I'm going up to the ranch."

"You have a ranch?" Sandy blurted as she felt her eyes widened.

"No," Sister Betty said. "Friends of mine do. They breed and raise Appaloosa horses."

"Where is this ranch?" Sandy was intrigued.

"Up in Colorado. A working ranch. You're not going up there to sit on your butt, and that's why I needed to know if you could be trusted to pitch in. These girls work five days a week teaching. They have the horses to take care of and breed, and during the winter, they run a day ski area with a lodge on weekends." Sister Betty took a breath and continued. "They have a hard time doing it all, but they're happy doing it. I think you can help. Besides, I need your pickup."

Sandy wasn't a bit surprised that Sister Betty had an ulterior motive. She was getting to know her pretty well. But she didn't know exactly what the wily nun intended. "Why do we need the pickup?"

"My VW's too small for all the stuff I want to take this weekend, but your pickup with its camper shell will be just right."

Sandy learned too that they'd be going over Wolf Creek Pass, a steep two-lane road with seven to eight percent grade along much of it. It could be tricky if there was snow, especially for a VW. Her Jeep would be much more reliable. A few years later country musician C. W. McCall's song made the pass famous by describing it as "thirty-seven miles o'hell … which is up on the Great Divide."

The weekend came and Sandy left her dog, Candy, with a friend and headed off with Sister Betty. They drove Sandy's loaded truck the three hundred forty miles through Farmington, New Mexico, across the state line up through Durango, over Wolf Creek Pass—without a hitch, past the Great Sand Dunes, then Route 69 to the ranch.

Sister Betty had told Sandy some about Clara and Margaret, and so she wasn't surprised by how warmly they greeted their friend. Nor was she surprised by the warmth and kindness they showed her as they met and welcomed her. A friend of Sister Betty's was indeed a friend of theirs.

That warmth was a good memory when she woke up the next morning in a very cold house. Thirty-eight to forty degrees, she estimated, feeling it all the way to her bones. She heard someone building a fire and stayed put for a bit under the six or eight blankets she'd piled on over the flannel sheets. Even with all that, she'd still been cold, and she'd covered all of herself except her nostrils so she could breathe during the night. It was really cold.

But morning chores awaited. She knew Sister Betty expected her to help, and she wanted to. Leaving the cold comfort of her bed, Sandy dressed and cautiously descended the narrow, steep, curved staircase to the three small rooms below. Sure enough, the fire she'd heard someone building was blazing in the rock fireplace, warming the living and dining areas. The wood cook stove in the kitchen was also doing its share to generate heat, and in the process, sent out the heavenly smell of brewing coffee. The coffee was even more heavenly to taste. Sandy thought it must have been made by an angel.

After helping feed horses, dogs, chickens, and filling the wood box, she took a better look around the place. She could easily imagine pioneers living in the old log house, and in a way, she thought, that's just what Clara and Margaret were. Pioneers, living close to the land, being where they wanted to be, despite the hard work and inconveniences.

She was standing in the weaning pen when Margaret joined her. The ranchers had weaned all the foals by this time of year, so the pen was full. Sandy knew nothing about horses. Chickens, yes, because her father raised them. In the dairyland area of upstate New York, she'd known only Holstein cattle and, of course, chickens. True, Margaret and Clara had three milk cows, Mikey, James, and Harold. They provided the needed milk, and cream that would become butter. But important as they were, they weren't the main feature by any means. This was a horse ranch, and ever-curious Sandy wanted to learn what she could about horses.

The weaning pen held a couple of them with spots all over. "I've never seen horses with spots like that," Sandy said.

Jamming her hands down into her jeans pocket and looking at Sandy with twinkling brown eyes, Margaret confided in her. "Clara's and my project is we're trying to breed the spots out of the Appaloosas."

Sandy, who later acknowledged she "didn't know for shit," thought she was telling the truth. Margaret continued. "Oh, they need to look like all the other horses. The spots have to go."

Sandy bought it. How was she to know the Appaloosa breed was especially prized for its flashy markings, those spots being the basis of that cherished flashiness? That if you don't get the required eye, skin and coat patterns, then you don't have an Appaloosa that people would recognize by sight? That they can be a solid color with just a white blanket over their hindquarters? That there are hardly ever any two that look exactly alike? And she certainly didn't have a clue that the color patterns went back a couple thousand years in China, also quite a way back in Persia and Norway. And in this country, the type had been bred by the Nez Perce and named for the Palouse River that runs through Northern Idaho. That the term A Palouse horse had evolved to Appaloosa. She didn't know there was a big demand for these horses because of their even-tempered dispositions and trustworthiness.[1] She didn't know for shit. But she would learn.

The weekend sped by. She and Sister Betty cooked, did dishes, tossed hay bales down from the loft, and helped make butter. Clara did the milking, the old separator did its job, and Sandy and Sister Betty churned. Margaret repaired the chicken house and fences. They all worked hard, and Sandy appreciated knowing she'd been of use. That was reward enough but, in addition, they went home with the same kind of goodies Sandy had seen Sister Betty bring back—some of that luscious butter they'd helped make, venison, frozen chickens, eggs. She couldn't wait to go back to the ranch.

After a few more trips with Sister Betty, Sandy worked up the nerve to ask Clara and Margaret something that had been on her mind a lot, something she really wanted. "If I have time off and Sister Betty doesn't, could I come here by myself?"

"You bet," the ranchers said in complete accord. And thus a long friendship took another solid step.

Along with beginning to learn a whole lot about horses, Sandy also learned more about how Sister Betty's life overlapped with Mac's and

---

1 From Clara Reida interview with Jaye Zola, March 3, 2014, and *http://www.appaloosa.com/ association/history.htm*

therefore with Margaret's. How Mac and Margret's connection had stayed strong, with Mac and her friend Phyllis coming to the ranch summers when they could to help out. She noticed how friends, old and new, wanted to contribute however they could to Margaret and Clara's success with their ranch. Sure money was short with bills to pay and everything going back into the ranch, the to-do list never ending, only continually expanding, but their friends were eager to pitch in when they could.

Sandy also learned how steadfast the ranchers were when it came to friends and working through problems. On her first trip there without Sister Betty, she took her dog, Candy, along. Candy got along just fine with the other dogs, Ugly or Ug for short, Bashful, and Margaret's old Weimaraner, Smokey. But the chickens didn't fare so well. Candy killed the ones she could get her mouth on before Sandy could stop her. Rather than raise a fuss, Margaret, a genius with dogs, started working with Candy, as did Sandy. Eventually the dog would leave the free-ranging chickens alone and could, therefore, be allowed to be free-ranging herself.

Sandy felt comfortable with both Clara and Margaret but to her, the friendship with Clara seemed to develop more easily and naturally. It progressed a little more slowly with Margaret. She was in awe of this take-charge person who, while friendly and appreciative of Sandy's interest in and help on the ranch, maintained a bit more distance. Margaret was a little trickier to read and to know how to respond to.

Respect for Margaret came easily, no question. Sandy marveled at how she, who was in charge of all the building, could work out in her head exactly what was needed and how to put it all together. Sandy, Clara, and anyone else around, would just follow Margaret's precise directions—nail these things here, those things there—and all would come out just fine. As it did with the friendship, over time.

TOWARD SUMMER OF 1974, SANDY GOT A CALL FROM HER MOM, HELEN, telling her Sandy's dad was seriously ill. Describing the tough spot she was in, Helen said, "I don't like leaving your dad alone while I'm at work, and you know it'll be a couple of years before I can retire."

Over the pounding of her heart, Sandy heard her mom ask, "Is there any way you could come back and help?"

"Of course, I'll come help," she told her. "I have to tie up things here, but that won't take long. I'll be there as soon as I can."

Back in New York, Sandy completed her Bachelor of Science degree. Then in 1976, Helen did retire and could take on the care of her husband herself. Sandy was free to return to Shiprock.

She was happy to be back in the west with her friends and doing the work she loved. But in only a year her father's steadily declining health called her back to the northeast. He died in November of 1978, but not before Sandy made a promise to him, one that came from her heart. "Wherever I am, Mom will have a home. It won't be in New York, because I'd like to go back to New Mexico. But wherever it is, Mom will have a home."

Helen didn't want to move immediately after her husband passed, and Sandy respected that. She knew her mom believed that leaving a house right away where you've lost someone can interfere with going through your grief. Because Helen wanted to stay in the house long enough to settle her feelings, they stayed the winter, waiting till spring of 1979 to put the hundred-year-old farmhouse on the market.

But six months after her father died, another blow fell. Sandy's beloved Candy had a mini-stroke and had to be put down. Heartbroken, Sandy still carried on, as she knew she had to. But it was a challenge, emotionally and even physically, given the climate she found herself back in.

To Sandy, the winter of 1978-79 was about the worst she'd ever seen. One Canadian front after another came through bringing temperatures of thirty and forty below zero. February brought severe sleet storms. If the thermometer registered as high as zero, she and Helen considered themselves lucky. But warmth came by way of friends, especially letters and cards from Clara. And then the phone call from Clara telling her she would have a puppy for Sandy when she came back west. Friends. People who know just what's needed.

Sandy felt heartened by Clara's thoughtfulness, her spirits buoyed by the idea of having a pup from good, old Ug, the smartest dog on the ranch. Ug had a habit of stopping by every year to see a neighbor dog a half-mile up the road from the ranch. Because according to Clara, a big, mean dog had moved into the neighborhood, this would probably be Ug's last litter.

Now Sandy's only worry was that they wouldn't sell the house in time to get the puppy. Again, Clara reassured her. She and Margaret would take care of the pup till Sandy was in a position to take her.

We expect our lives to overlap within family, to give and get support when needed, and that's what was going on in Sandy and Helen's case. Sandy had made that promise to her dad, and she was going to keep it. But it wasn't only about honoring the promise; Sandy and Helen enjoyed each other, and they wanted each other to be happy. Now the question before them was just *where* were they going to be happy?

If you've ever had the opportunity to begin life anew, you know how exciting and daunting it can be. Finding the right place, your niche, your spot is this vast land can seem overwhelming. And when there are two of you, the challenge is, well, doubled. But Sandy knew she had to follow her heart, a heart that longed for the west. Helen was willing to check it out, so that's where they headed first in the search for their new home.

In June of 1979, they flew to Farmington, New Mexico with plans to continue on to Pueblo, Colorado once they'd had some time in Shiprock. They arranged the trip so Helen could see a little of both New Mexico and Colorado, two of Sandy's most beloved places. As it turned out, having more than one place in mind proved fortunate. To Sandy's surprise, Helen hated New Mexico. She found the prevalence of desert brown and lack of verdant hues appalling. The friends, she loved. The scenery she didn't. After good visits in unacceptable country, they were off to Colorado.

Clara met them at the Pueblo airport and drove them through the tree-lined streets, out past the high prairie and into the Wet Mountains. Helen breathed in the dry, crisp air and exclaimed, "Oh, I could live here.

This is green enough. And there are trees!"

"Fine with me," Sandy replied, and it was fine. "But I'm not going to spend another winter in New York!"

Now that a possibility had opened, Sandy wanted to relax and be with her friends. She knew the search to pin down exactly where they would settle would be on soon enough. For now she wanted to meet her new puppy and enjoy the ranch.

Dogs held high rank with Sandy, as they did with Margaret and Clara. Often in my quest to learn more about the lives of these friends, dates would be identified by which dog was around. "Hmm, I think that's when Smokey was still with us." Or "That happened right after Bash came along." This was so with horses, too. Animals were key markers, touchstones in these eventful lives, and Sandy was eager to meet the little one she'd named Ason, Navajo for "old lady," Ug's puppy, the cute, fluffy pup in those photos Clara had sent. The doggie she would call Ace. Her dog.

Entering the house, first thing Sandy came face to face with a gangly juvenile pooch. Helen saw it, too. She opened, then closed, then opened her mouth again and pushing it away from her, she cried, "That's one ugly dog! I hope that's not Ason!"

"Yep. That's Ason," Clara confirmed.

"Couldn't you have gotten something cuter?" Helen asked.

Poor Ason. She had been a darling, cuddly pup. But now she was a skinny, awkward adolescent. Homely, yes, but lovable. Soon she would grow into her adult self. A beautiful, smart, loving adult self. She, Sandy, and Helen would be together for twelve years, and the dog would be a built-in reflection of their bond to Singing Acres Ranch. But at the moment, she was not cute, and a far cry from beautiful.

Despite the young dog's awkward stage, Sandy was grateful for the Ason connection and also touched by Margaret's and Clara's invitation for her and her mother to stay at the ranch until they found a home. Knowing the two rancher friends understood the challenges of such a move, Sandy also felt immense relief from the offer. They had to return to New York first, put the house on the market, pack up. But they would return within a few months. And the big move, half-a-continent shift was made much easier by the steadfast support of these two women and their ready-made network of friends. In big and little matters, pals were there to help.

When the time came, friend Sherry Campbell met the moving van and directed the unloading of the Greenes' belongings into the old ski lodge. Sandy had gotten to know Sherry, who lived a mile down the road in the old schoolhouse, well. Sherry had moved to the area in 1972 when she'd married Jim, soon becoming part of the ranch's life.

Sandy knew that every weekday for years Sherry had fed Maude, the ranchers' orphaned workhorse, while they were off to their teaching jobs. She appreciated how Sherry felt about learning so much from both Margaret and Clara. In Sherry's case, that included how to take care of animals, which she hadn't known as a girl growing up back east. They'd even given her a mare, one that went on to have three colts.

Another friend, Realtor Dona Kenline began looking for a house for Sandy and Helen. And then Sandy found a job working afternoons at the Florence hospital. The commute from Singing Acres wasn't long, about twenty-five miles each way, and it was scenic. But in bad weather, the narrow, steep and winding road through the Hardscrabble Canyon portion could be tricky.

One evening when she was late getting off work, a blizzard moved in, dense fat snowflakes collecting into drifts in no time. Driving Clara's Subaru across the eleven miles of prairie between Florence and Wetmore, Sandy watched the accumulation growing ever heavier and deeper. Past Wetmore and a few miles up the canyon, it was almost obscuring the car's headlights.

Having been caught in numerous blizzards, I can see Sandy leaning forward to peer through the whiteness, feel how her muscles tensed as her hands gripped the steering wheel while keeping a measured, cautious pace. I can imagine her exhaling with relief as she rounded one particularly sharp curve and saw a big, slow-moving snowplow ahead.

Glad to be in its wake, the fact that the going seems even more snail-like mattered little because the snowplow made the drive decidedly less treacherous. Arriving at the ranch around 1:00 a.m., she must have been exhilarated. The terrifying drive was behind her. She was home and safe.

Inside she found an anxious and exhausted Helen and Clara, who, despite waiting up, had hoped she would stay in town and not risk that drive. They'd had no way of knowing where she was, and the uncertainty had been awful. Sandy, elated by the safe conclusion to her stressful adventure, wanted to laugh and joke, as I would have. But Helen and Clara, drained from hours of their anxious waiting, were having none of that. Trudging off to bed, Helen grumbled, "Don't you ever do that again!"

The incident brought more clarity to Helen about where they should live, and she was quick to tell Sandy about it. "We can't live up here. You can't live in the mountains, not with your having to drive in conditions like this. It would give me the big one!"

The process of elimination had begun. Helen also ruled out Penrose, about thirty miles northeast of the ranch, because of wind and dust. Canon City, thirteen miles west of Penrose, had too many old people driving around, and that wasn't safe. "I could, however, live in Florence," she said, referring to the nice little town between those other two, the town in which Sandy worked.

As the search for a home went on, Helen was happy to take care of the Singing Acres house. Sandy knew how much Clara and Margaret loved Helen's efforts and coming home to a clean, warm house, dinner and a fresh pot of coffee after a long day of teaching and after-school activities. The arrangement worked well, with everyone doing her part on the ranch. Sandy felt she learned many a thing she wouldn't have otherwise. One in particular was how to butcher a hog. Sometimes she'd come home, and if it wasn't too cold, the carcass would be hanging in the barn. Imagine coming in to find, as she did once, a note that said, "Don't take a shower. There's a hog's head in the tub."

Yet issues did come up, as they do when people live close to each other. Habits, lifetime patterns, strengths, faults and foibles have more opportunities to appear. And with two strong-willed people in the house such as Helen and Margaret, those opportunities could prove memorable. Helen, as outspoken as Margaret, didn't hesitate in calling things the way she saw them. Margaret, being so competent in cooking and many other matters, could be a bit on the bossy side, and probably more so when she'd had herself a drink or two. Having experienced both Helen's candor and Margaret's resolute supervision, I have little trouble picturing a particular, telling encounter between those two that happened one winter's night, as this one did.

It was evening, and Helen was preparing dinner as usual on the wood-burning stove. From the next room Sandy saw that Margaret hovered in the small kitchen, advising Helen on cooking dinner. Her hands around her coffee mug, Margaret kept getting in Helen's path from counter to stove.

Finally, Helen had had it. Sandy watched in horror as her mom turned on Margaret, still holding the knife and fork she'd been working with, and shouted, "Damn it! I am cooking dinner. Go sit on your ass in the living room. You are drunk and you don't know what you're doing. And you're not going to ruin my meal!"

Margaret knew she had met her match, and that became even more evident as Helen went on. "You think I'm afraid of you? I'm not. Other people may be afraid of you, but I am not."

Mumbling, Margaret went off to sit in front of the fire as Helen prepared the meal. That she did so, Sandy thought, was some measure of Margaret's regard for Helen. The two of them liked teasing and taunting each other, but they also had head-on clashes. Underneath it all, though, Sandy knew they deeply appreciated and cared for each other. She thought that maybe that esteem and love made it possible for them to have those go-rounds and then carry on as buddies. They knew they could blow up and trust the other not to hold it against the other. It didn't seem like denial in any way. It seemed like two fiercely independent, outspoken people asserting themselves with each other. Thank goodness, Sandy thought, for the times when they laughed like crazy together.

With Realtor friend Dona's help, Sandy and Helen found just the right house in Florence, and in January of 1980, they moved. It amused and touched Sandy when Clara, upon learning about the house, said, "No way! I can't let you go! I don't want to come home to a cold house and no coffee." Sandy and Helen had lived with them for three months by that time.

Mother and daughter would live in the Florence house together for thirty-two years, until Helen's death in 2012. But for many years, some important things didn't change. On weekends and days off, at the ranch, Sandy and Helen continued to help get wood for cooking and heating. And because of Margaret's duties as cook combined with a longer commute to work, Sandy helped Clara with the horses, including the foaling. Given her nursing experience and Clara's knowledge of horses, the two made a good team, especially with Margaret pitching in when needed.

When a foal was expected, Sandy would go to the ranch after work, or if it was her day off, she and Helen would go stay over. Sandy, Clara, and Margaret took turns checking on the mother-to-be throughout the night. Clara did the 10:00 check, leaving a note, "Everything okay at 10 p.m." Then Margaret at midnight, and Sandy at 2:00 a.m. Each dutifully wrote whether the mare was sleeping or if there were no signs of labor before going back to bed. Then Clara would be up again at 4:00, starting fires in the stove and fireplace and making coffee. When one of them would find a newborn foal, shouts of, "We've got a baby! We've got a baby!" rang out.

Everyone had to go see the foal right away, even the dogs. After a proper greeting, Margaret would then make a pot of coffee, and Clara and Sandy would spend the rest of the night monitoring, to make sure the baby was nursing

The seven to nine foals a year meant a lot of careful watching. With multiple indicators to be on the lookout for as the baby developed— if it could stand, if the baby and mother bonded, whether it was nursing, if the mother was producing sufficient milk, whether there were respiratory problems, and other signs—the ranchers and their friend were plenty busy. And if something wasn't going well, then they were even busier.

A number of years later this teamwork would produce other important results when the ranch saw an outbreak of the red scours, clostridium-perfingens, which is a potentially fatal form of diarrhea in foals. Sandy's knowledge of medical terms came in handy and she and Clara worked to figure out just what they needed for a vaccination program. They spent many a night with the horses in the barn, many an hour researching what might be helpful. Sandy didn't balk at any task when the vet came, becoming, as Clara later said, a really good vet assistant. With help from the vet and their combination of experience and knowledge, eventually they created a vaccination program that worked.

Being part of the Singing Acres Ranch family felt so right and natural to Sandy, and she knew her mom shared that feeling. What good fortune that their lives had come to overlap with Clara's and Margaret's in that way. Those two had opened their home and their hearts to them. They, in turn, were happy to give back when they could, which was often. Over time they shared life stories, and their friendship created many more that resonated long into the future.

11

Sisters & Friends
1988 – 1991

Ialways smile when I think about their first meeting. Irony often makes me smile, and when my sister was involved, my smile could only get bigger. In this case, even with their suspicions about anyone from that commune Stillpoint, Clara and Margaret really didn't know what they were getting into when they agreed to talk with Susan, who was seeking advice on a matter they knew something about. After the initial phone call, despite their preconceived notions they agreed to help. They figured they'd talk to "that person from that place" and be done with it.

But it turned out differently. Not only would they not be done with it, but their meeting would affect all three profoundly and, eventually it would affect me.

It started with a horse, one of several Susan had at Stillpoint, the place having fallen under her care in 1985 when friend and associate Gia-fu Feng died. Gia-fu had been an uncommon figure in the area, one that Margaret and Clara had had their doubts about. Now in 1988, Susan was there, living in a rustic cabin called the tea house, trying to make improvements on the neglected land. Among the horses was Farasya, an Arabian mare and descendant of Gia-fu's stallion, Kalahari. Farasaya was seriously ill and several people had suggested that Susan get in touch with Clara, widely known for her skills with horses. Susan called to see if they could talk in person.

I can picture that auspicious morning in 1988 as, at the appoint-ed time, the two ranchers watched a pickup head up their drive and park across from the corral. A slender woman in jeans and floppy shirt emerged, long straight hair falling loosely down her back. They thought as one, "She sure looks like one of 'those people.'"

Their experience of "those people" had been brief, but with all they'd heard beforehand about the unusual lifestyle at Stillpoint, Clara's one quick stop there a few years ago, had instantly underscored rumors about scantily clad or unclad folks in and around a hot tub in which that Chinese man sat, about the seemingly closed nature of the group.

She and Margaret had stopped by to give a sheepskin they'd come across to a woman who lived at Stillpoint. They'd met when the woman had been walking by the ranch and stopped to ask for a drink of water. She'd talked about how she'd really like to have a sheepskin. Then through a friend, they acquired one and they wanted to give it to the woman. But the people who met them when they drove in were unfriendly, yelling at them to go away.

The encounter had unsettled Clara and fortified her misgivings. Now, three years after Gia-fu Feng had passed on, here was another woman from that place, and although Susan hadn't been there at the time of the visit, Clara had that association. Still, it was horses the young woman wanted to talk about, and so they would talk with her and find out what was going on. And, of course, they would help if they could.

It wasn't until several years later, after Susan died, that they told me how surprised they'd been about her, their reservations melting in minutes. They'd found nary a hint of the stereotypical hippie type they'd suspected populated Stillpoint. From the very beginning, Susan's straightforward and articulate manner reassured them. Her real concern for Farasaya and the lengths to which she'd already gone on her behalf erased any remaining reserve. They were three people who cared about an animal, about a horse, this horse. And they were three people, they would soon come to realize, who had much more in common than that.

Each held views generally unencumbered by convention and each lived lives shaped and often buoyed by challenge, some of which they would soon experience together. Their initial exchange formed the beginnings of a new friendship, one that would continue and deepen for the rest of Susan's short life.

Margaret and Clara appreciated that Susan was a civil rights attorney whose interests lay in helping those who otherwise wouldn't get help. They were wowed by the fact that she was a former Army captain, a scholar of Asian studies, an independent and determined woman, and voracious reader. That she was also a kind and caring soul fit her right in with those two. They knew what it was to forge one's own way in the face of barriers and orthodox expectations, and Susan knew that they knew. They understood the need to reach out to others, to create a sense of community where they could, to challenge their own minds, to appreciate literature, music, beauty—and animals. They knew how important it was to just keep going forward. Most of all, they knew the value of friendship, and here was a new one, a surprise one, just beginning. Susan felt that, too, and she soon told me about it. She was delighted to have found them.

Clara tended to most things horse-related at the ranch and it had been her reputation with horses that had brought Susan to her. Although their conversation could've gone in many different directions, as it later would, Farasaya's condition held much of the focus that morning.

So far Susan hadn't found anyone who could give an adequate diagnosis of the mare's condition, including the vet. Farasaya's pregnancy meant that whatever was going on most likely would affect the foal, so that made the situation even more serious. Clara agreed to keep Farasaya at the ranch, observe her, treat her.

In the end, despite Clara's good work, the foal didn't make it, and neither did Farasaya, who was thought to have had cancer.

In helping Susan with Farasaya, Clara and Margaret found a friend, but they also found that Farasaya had brought trouble to the ranch. It came in the form of bacteria called Clostridium-Perfingens Types C and D. Although it could be found in healthy animals, Clostridial bacteria can multiply and "cause disease and death by the production of enterotoxins and subsequent toxemia."[1] It was deadly to foals, and at that time there

---

[1]http://vads.vetmed.vt.edu/demos/Education/display.cfm?ShowMyFile=Organisms/ClPerfFS.htm

was no equine vaccine they knew of.

The ranchers knew that both types of clostridium can form spores that will live for long periods in the soil. One solution called for covering all the area with two feet of fresh soil, but in their case that meant a lot of territory. The impracticality of it led Clara to look for another answer. Aided by nurse friend Sandy, and with guidance from veterinarians Doctors Gerald Shiner and Lisa Eskridge, they first tried using a vaccine that had been developed for cattle[2]. Initially they used it on the foals, to no avail. Then Dr. Shiner suggested that since the vaccine was given to breeding cows, maybe they should test it on the mares. They did, and it worked.

Next they began immunizing the mares just as they would for sleeping sickness or anything else: giving them a primary shot, then six weeks or so later, another shot of the same thing, and every year after, a booster.

Their program prevented Clostridium-perfingens from starting in the foals, a big nightmare banished from the ranch, and from other ranches that learned about their discovery. And some time later, Clara, Sandy and Margaret all breathed a sigh of relief when a drug company came up with a solution to another problem, an oral treatment for foals less than twelve hours old that would prevent e-coli, white scours, a terrible diarrhea.

Who could've known that Susan's search for help with Farasaya would have such far-reaching effects, or that such a dark cloud would, indeed, have a silver lining?

The response to help Susan came naturally to Margaret and Clara, and doing so undeniably brought other problems. But it wasn't the only time the ranchers had encountered problems in their efforts to do what they felt was right. At the time of their meeting Susan, the two were embroiled in a lawsuit that had grown out of their concern for horses at a neighboring ranch. It started a couple of years earlier when

---

2 CDT: Clostridium-perfingens Type C and D anti-toxins

Margaret and Clara had become increasingly upset about the condition in which they had, year after year, seen the rancher's horses. And even more so because they knew these horses were well worked on tourist trips into the Sangre de Cristo Mountains.

The poor things were always in sight when they drove down the road past them, and the sight was unsettling. Bone thin, unresponsive, vacant-eyed, the creatures naturally aroused their sympathy, and their ill treatment provoked their anger. Ranchers know that starving one's horses is a criminal offense, and so with justice for the horses in mind, they pursued it.

They knew that friend Pat Schulz had registered a complaint with the sheriff's office that January of 1987. Pat and her husband, Tom, were friends who knew horses well, and the sight of those poor horses horrified Pat. When nothing seemed to happen with Pat's complaint, they wrote a letter to the District Attorney asking for action, detailing the problems with the horses. When no action came, six months later in July, the case was thrown out.

Sometimes justice seems elusive, and it did in this case. The problem was that although anyone who knew what they were looking at could see the horses were starving, proving it required an autopsy. Even an expert, a veterinarian, might be able to say a horse looks malnourished, but s/he can't confirm it without that autopsy. The problem could be a parasite or something else entirely, so to say definitely that the horses were starving without such proof fell into the realm of conjecture. Ultimately, because of the difficulty of proof, the possibility of a criminal case was dismissed.

But the neighbor lashed back. He filed suit against Clara, Margaret, and Pat, although the claims against Pat were ultimately dismissed at the mid-point of the jury trial because she'd filed formally rather than through letters or calls. He claimed libel, for their letters and complaints to the sheriff's office, the health department, and Humane Society. He seemed particularly affronted by Margaret's nicknaming his ranch "Starvation Acres." He also charged malicious prosecution, asserting that the claims against him had been fraudulently filed, along with outrageous conduct, stating that the three had "continually harassed and attempted to interfere and harm the business of the Plaintiff."[3] It was clear that despite knowing they were in the right, Clara and Margaret needed legal help.

Margaret stopped by a law office in Canon City to find that help, asking for a referral for a woman attorney. That referral was Brenda Jackson, a young attorney in town. After an initial after-school visit from Margaret, on April 26, 1988, they had their first meeting with her. In Brenda they found another connection, another recognition of a kindred spirit. They were instant friends. They hired the young attorney, and in that attorney's words, "We were off to the races."

With the September court date less than six months away, Susan offered to help. Margaret and Clara felt consumed by the lawsuit, by its absurdity in their eyes—a distraction from the still-starving horses, by the time and attention it was taking, and their very real disquiet about the outcome. A lot was on the line. Brenda was the only attorney for the defense, and there was much to be done. Susan, having prosecuted and defended in military, civil, and tribal courts, was a veteran of lawsuits. Her licenses to practice, however, included New Mexico, where she'd had a private practice, and North Dakota, where she worked with friend and attorney Vance Gillette, but not in Colorado, where she'd only recently returned.

Susan made a call to Brenda, and they had what was to be the first of many talks. She told Brenda, "Margaret and Clara are fine with it, if I can help. I can't practice law in the state, but I can do a lot of other things. I can interview witnesses, do investigations, serve subpoenas, and write motions if you need any of this."

"Absolutely. That would be wonderful!" said a relieved and delighted Brenda.

Susan did much of this legwork, meeting with potential witnesses, serving subpoenas, and doing all the other tasks she'd offered to do. It proved a huge help to Brenda and of course, to Clara and Margaret.

---

3 Case No. 88CV33, Custer County District Court; TRIAL DISCLOSURE CERTIFICATE OF PLAINTIFF, Jan. 19, 1988.

They were a team.

The trial was set for September 11, 1989. It was a four-day, district civil court, jury trial, with the six jurors selected from the small community of Westcliffe. Reflecting on it years later, Brenda said, "If they didn't know Margaret and Clara personally, they had heard of them. So you just make sure they haven't heard negative things, or think bad things, and you roll the dice."

Brenda did indeed roll the dice, and twenty-five years later, she told me in more detail just how they landed.

On the other side was attorney J.C. Martin III, who went by the name of Pit Martin. He too was relatively new to the business with perhaps one year more experience than Brenda's scant four.

The witness lists for both plaintiff and defendants were long. Ranchers, neighbors, health department officials, State Animal Protection official, Parks and Rec Department, sheriff's department, and more. Susan had served thirteen subpoenas for the defendants, and the plaintiff had called twenty-four more. A number of horse experts testified, including the veterinarian for the plaintiff's horses. He confirmed that vets wouldn't say a horse is starving to death without a necropsy. He went as far as to say horses can *look* malnourished, but that a vet won't say they *are* malnourished. This is when Brenda told Margaret that they needed pictures because she didn't think they had good enough ones. With good photos, she reasoned, maybe at least they could get the vet to say these horses *looked* malnourished.

Margaret undertook the mission with her usual aplomb. That very evening, under the cover of dusk, she sneaked up to the corrals at the neighboring ranch and climbed over the rails in order to get as close as possible. She aimed her Polaroid camera and got a number of good shots. Satisfied, she started to leave and climbed back over the rails. About that time, the wind came up, caught the photos, blew them out of her hand and back into the corrals. Undaunted, Margaret climbed back in, retrieved the pictures, and sneaked out again, the requested evidence safely in her pocket.

The next day, when Brenda wondered how to explain how she'd gotten the pictures, Margaret said, "I'll just tell them the truth. I don't care." But, as it turned out, an explanation proved unnecessary.

The trial continued. The plaintiff testified about how traumatized he was from being charged with a crime. "Our horses are free-range horses," he said, suggesting that even if there are six feet of snow and their water is frozen solid, these horses can scratch for and find food—theoretically. He admitted, that other than the pasture, they didn't feed them in the winter.

A school bus driver testified. She'd had to stop the bus because the horses were on the road trying to find food. She noted how the horses' backbones were protruding about two inches above their haunches because they had no flesh; how their hip bones were protruding. How the horses were emaciated.

Neighbors and others testified about Margaret and Clara's sound ranching practices, about their good character, about their contributions to the community. More wanted to be called, but Brenda had to limit the numbers, which had already grown large.

Brenda would remember how the plaintiff tried to stigmatize Clara and Margaret with statements like this: "Well, nobody takes care of their horses like Singing Acres Ranch. They overfeed, they pamper their horses."

Amused by the horse-pamperer hyperbole, the team for the defendants knew how horses were fed at Singing Acres was far from the plaintiff's standard for how to raise and care for horses. The contrast raised a good question. What was a popularly recognized standard, and how could such a standard be posed in court? Brenda, Clara, Margaret, Pat and Susan conferred.

As a result of their deliberations, Brenda brought in a 4H book on how a fifth-grader raises a horse. She took the jury through it, page by page. How much water do you give your horse? How do you take care of it in the winter? How much hay do you give it every day? The 4H book did indeed offer a standard, and a clear one that a grade-school student could understand. Brenda could tell the jury clearly appreciated the concrete and widely-accepted information as they followed the numerous details.

Additionally, the final straw, the one that broke the back of the plaintiff's argument, even with the veterinarian's testimony about the necessity of an autopsy, came with Brenda's use of that same veterinarian's books on horse nutrition. Beginning with information about blood chemistry, citing signs of how to determine if a horse has nutritional needs, Brenda read to the jury from the books the vet had lent her. She also had stacks of handouts from Colorado State University's equine program, provided by Clara's former student Melanie Camper Fall, who then worked at the Extension office. Every detail and bit of information that could be used got used, everything that would help the jury understand that there were ways to tell what horses need and when they aren't getting it, Brenda read. She watched the jurors take it all in.

Then came the summing up for Pit and Brenda. It had been a long trial with abundant information, and it took them much of the morning to complete their arguments. Next came the jury's instructions, after which the jurors adjourned for their deliberations. This was an anxiety-provoking time, particularly for those whose lives didn't revolve around trials. Clara, Margaret and Pat were relieved when, by the end of the day, the jury reappeared to return the verdict.

They watched as the jury members filed in and took their seats. Susan later told me how she held her breath as the judge asked the foreman for their findings and he stood to read, "We, the jury, find for the defendant Margaret Locarnini and against the plaintiff ... on his claim of libel." And so it went for each charge, for each defendant. The jury returned one hundred percent in Clara and Margaret's favor. Susan exhaled and the whole SAR team smiled.

They smiled even more when the judge awarded them two-thirds of their attorney fees. Ultimately, some of the remaining fee came from the opposing attorney personally. Best of all, they would later learn the plaintiff was feeding his horses well, perhaps even up to SAR standards.

Two and a half decades later, Brenda said, "Every time I think about it, it cracks me up. That trial was probably the most fun I've ever had in the courtroom on a case. It was so much fun, and a lot of it was because of the attitude of Margaret, Clara and Pat through the whole thing. They were so certain they were going to win, they never had any doubt. They did the right thing. They just stuck to their principles from beginning to end."

Brenda also loved working with Susan on the case and developing a treasured connection. "I'd go up to the hermitage [Stillpoint] and we'd sit and drink tea and discuss the facts and talk about the witnesses and trial presentation. We would talk for hours. She was my behind-the-scenes attorney who was helping me figure this all out even if she couldn't conduct the examinations. Preparing witnesses and serving subpoenas and laughing at it with the rest of us."

I wasn't at the trial, but I remember Susan telling me about it. She was completely dedicated to doing what needed to be done because of her passion for the justice of it. That it affected people whom she'd come to love propelled her further. She would leave no detail unattended, allowing herself to be consumed by doing whatever needed to be done. This is how she was.

It made her happy to help people she cared about, to aid in righting wrongs. This was why she'd entered law school after finishing her Master's Degree at the California Institute of Asian Studies. She saw it as a way to help. She, Margaret, and Clara had lots in common. And now, in Brenda, she had another new friend who wanted to work for good. And soon they had another chance to work together in saving Stillpoint from development.

Susan had done most of the legwork and research for the case herself, but again, because Susan wasn't licensed in Colorado, and also because attorneys know that "only a fool acts as his own attorney," Brenda represented Susan in court. The result, as I recounted in the introduction, was the public auction Clara urged me to attend. As I drove by Singing Acres Ranch that morning on the way to it, to my sister, I thought of circles—the circle of trials, of personal decisions, and mainly of sisters and friends.

THERE WAS MORE THAT HAPPENED FOR SUSAN, MARGARET AND CLARA in those years between 1989, with the trial, and 1991, when Susan died. They met in 1988, and not long after that, Susan became part of the family. She stayed at Singing Acres many nights at Clara and Margaret's invitation, and sometimes at their urging.

They were concerned for her living in the tea house since the cabin was out of the way and not insulated. Eventually, they designated a bedroom for her at the ranch, and she often slept there, especially when the temperature dropped and the snow was deep. But she had her affection for Stillpoint and her work on the improvements in forestry and restoring the many huts sprinkled around the land, so there were times when she felt she needed to be there.

But there were many evenings at the ranch when, sitting around the old oak table, cup of coffee in one hand, cigarette in the other, Susan, Clara and Margaret would talk for hours about anything and everything—horses, books, Eastern philosophy, even some of the rape cases Susan had prosecuted while in the Army. Through laughter, serious discussion, or everyday chit chat, they shared who they were and what they were concerned about. According to Clara, Susan brought ideas into the conversation that would enrich and deepen their exchanges, ideas such as mindfulness and what that meant in one's everyday life. And she and Margaret would share stories that illuminated whatever the three happened to be talking about. A satisfying communion all the way around.

From what they each told me over the years, I have a good idea of how Susan was able to connect with Margaret on the closely held issues of one's inner demons. In my mind's eye, I can see Susan listening attentively as Margaret shared what she didn't often share with others. Susan's blue eyes soft and full of understanding, she perhaps suggested things for Margaret to consider, maybe a book that would help. Or a way of being quiet and letting thoughts come up to notice, to recognize, but not react to. Or someone else to talk with. I suspect Margaret figured Susan understood because she knew her own demons well enough, the drive to accomplish something good, to be good enough—be smart enough. Don't many of us have that one?

Then when Margaret wanted to own up to and check her drinking, Susan was there, a big support, along with Clara. Margaret must have known they were rooting for her, maybe nudging but not pushing. She knew most clearly of all they cared about her.

And there were the projects they worked on together. Susan delighted in telling me about the hunter's cookbook she was helping Margaret with. She'd type into the computer and save on floppy disks the recipes Margaret had honed for the venison or elk she'd hunted, the fish she caught, using the rosemary, thyme, sage and other herbs she'd grown. Using what was in the surroundings and what she could bring home mattered to her. And there was Susan, typing away, encouraging Margaret to come up with more. I still have those floppy disks, now undecipherable artifacts.

On some of those cold winter nights when Susan stayed over, she'd talk with Clara about the three hundred pages of Gia-fu's unfinished autobiography that Clara was editing. Susan wanted to organize and complete it, and Clara was doing yeoman's work on the editing. There was a job. Hundreds of pages of one thing after another, a granddaddy of a stream-of-consciousness manuscript. Some of those countless things interesting, but nothing in any chronological or other order so you could follow a story. Margaret would hear them laugh, then they'd tell her they'd just taken another big jump in time. When asked for examples, one of them would tell about an incident with Gia-fu's classics tutor in Shanghai in the 1920s that would follow a car accident in Big Sur in the 1960s—all in the same paragraph. And so it went.

The stories, Margaret and Clara figured, gave them a little bit of insight into who this strange-sounding and -looking character was. They'd been so suspicious of the small, unusual looking Chinese man, but they'd had to admit that if Susan had thought he was okay, there'd likely been more to him than they'd seen. Or had been willing to see. Of course, it was because of Gia-fu Feng that they knew Susan, because he'd left not only those writings, but his portion of Stillpoint in her hands. If it hadn't have been for that turn of events, they'd never have known each other, wouldn't have become friends. Really, more like sisters.

Susan was always slender, but during those last years, she grew more and more thin. She knew she wasn't well. She didn't feel well, and it wasn't only her lack of appetite, but a lack of energy, although watching her work made one doubt that symptom. She'd been told by at least one doctor that she likely had Lyme's Disease, probably based on her reports of fatigue and muscle and joint aches, along with occasional fever and chills. And she had stomachaches. But the prescribed antibiotics and other medications never seemed to help a whole lot.

Margaret and Clara encouraged her to eat, and she, in turn, tried. But her appetite was often not very good. Still, she would do the best she could while there, and then dutifully take home Margaret's canned beans, tomatoes, and other treasures and munch on them as much as she could.

When I visited, I would get to sample those treats myself. And I'd get to hear about what was going on at Singing Acres, and sometimes go there with Susan. Sometimes I'd visit her there. That's how it was.

In the end, all the good cooking, the encouragement to eat, the love and caring couldn't help Susan. The surprise diagnosis of metastasized stomach cancer after her first surgery took her away all too suddenly. When she died, Margaret and Clara were bereft. They'd lost a remarkable friend, having known her only three years, treasured years.

And then at the memorial gathering on a sunny hillside at Stillpoint, Clara offered to spread Susan's ashes, knowing there could be surprises among them, a bit of bone not completely turned to ash. Walking along beside her, I watched as the breeze took the ashes when she'd open her hand and lightly fling them, watched as they floated across the meadow. Some came to rest in the new spring grasses, others drifted toward the fir and ponderosa pines bordering the gently sloping field. Clara filled her hand again and again from the wooden box she held under her arm, each time offering its precious contents to the breeze. Taking slow, deliberate steps, she repeated the motions, her feet following a timeworn furrow, a remnant of the bygone days of dry-land farming on this land her friend, my sister, her sister, had loved. The place called Stillpoint.

12

The Rhythm of the Strands
1992-

SOME IMAGES ARE SO APT, SO EVOCATIVE, THEY JUST WON'T LET YOU go. One of those for me is from a book Susan and I read around 1988, a book we both loved. *A Yellow Raft in Blue Water* by Michael Dorris tells the story of three generations of Indian women, daughter/granddaughter, mother, and grandmother, whose lives, filled with struggles, are intricately intertwined through their kinship. The last line of the book, when the grandmother and the priest are sitting on the roof of her house on a cold New Year's Eve, is what grabbed me.

The grandmother let her warm blanket slip from her shoulders as she began an age-old task. When the priest asked what she was doing, she continued her motions, thinking, "As a man with cut hair, he did not identify the rhythm of three strands, the whispers of coming and going, of twisting and tying and blending, of catching and letting go, braiding."

Braiding. What a perfect image for Margaret and Clara with the people who came into and left their lives. Those "whispers of coming and going," just as Susan left their lives, our lives, just as we're left with the letting go. Just as others come in, who tie in, blend into the rhythm of life at Singing Acres. As you know by now, there were, and still are, many. The young attorney, Brenda Jackson, was one.

Brenda loved that Margaret and Clara just kind of took her in as family. If they hadn't heard from her for a while, maybe a month, Margaret would call. Home from work, Brenda would see a blinking light on her answering machine. She'd push the button, and Margaret's voice would come on. "Hi, It's the two old ladies up the hill. We're just wondering how you're doing, and if you're still alive or not."

Always that message, and she'd know it was time for a visit. She knew it meant Margaret was missing her and she needed to get her butt up to the ranch to see them. And off she'd go.

When, about 1996, Brenda had to have reconstructive knee surgery at St. Luke's Hospital in Denver, Margaret decided she'd take her. They travelled more than a hundred miles to be there, so they were eligible to stay the night at the hotel attached to St. Luke's.

Margaret had stayed at the hotel when she'd had her own knee surgery a few years earlier. I recall visiting in her hospital room after the operation, and particularly remember the unusual sight of this doer, this quintessence of activity, in bed, immobilized. Pain had sapped much of her strength and some of her feistiness, but not all. She joked with the nurse who came to check on her and cut short my expressions of sympathy. Instead, she teased me about being a "city girl," a favorite theme of hers when it came to me.

But she appreciated my coming to visit and said so. Admitting the pain was intense, she was relieved when the nurse came with the next dose of pain medication. She joked about that, too. So when Brenda told me Margaret was accompanying her, it made perfect sense. Margaret not only knew the routine, she knew it from the inside out, and she wanted Brenda to benefit from this knowledge. That was Margaret.

Shared experiences create the texture of our friendships. Several stories from Brenda's hospital trip became a favored strand in theirs. As soon as they arrived at the hospital's hotel, they checked into their room and went in search of a particular Indian restaurant they had in mind for dinner. They thought it would be close and easy to find, so they decided to walk. But it was neither and they walked seemingly endless blocks before they found it. And they found it closed.

Both were hungry and Brenda thought Margaret looked close to collapse. And although Margaret often growled, when she did this time, Brenda knew she meant it. "You're starving me to death! We have to find some place to eat."

The pressure to find food went up a notch. After a little more searching, they came upon a café that was open and busy enough to promise decent food. Brenda settled into her chair, relieved to give her knee a rest. She noticed Margaret examining the menu even before her bottom made contact with the chair. About the time it did, the fire alarm went off, and in the next instant, the waiters and manager were alerting customers, herding them outside. As they evacuated the building, they watched firefighters rush in to search for a gas leak, which they soon learned was to be a time-consuming mission.

With the hour growing late and the friends seriously hungry, they looked for another restaurant. They found one that was not closed nor being evacuated, and they ate. Meals can be memorable for many reasons, and for Brenda and Margaret, this meal would hold a prized spot.

Back at the hotel, despite the late hour, Margaret decided she needed a cigarette. She'd tried off and on over the years to stop smoking, but that had never lasted very long. Now, she told Brenda, she had to have one. Couldn't sleep if she didn't. Smoking wasn't allowed in the room or the lobby, so her only option was to descend the six floors and go outside.

Tired as she was, Brenda felt she needed to wait up for Margaret. Finally, when the lights did go off and the room grew still, they soon realized how paper-thin the hotel walls were. Strains of Broadway's best came to them as clearly as if they'd had their own TV on. Another voice, loud and off-key supplemented the broadcast. The woman in the next room belted out every tune right along with the performers. Brenda could imagine her twirling around and executing high kicks.

Giddy from exhaustion, they lay giggling and making sarcastic remarks for three hours while the woman sang Broadway melodies. For years after, every time they'd see one another, Margaret would start belting out a Broadway show tune and both would collapse with laughter.

Brenda was heartbroken when, in 2007, Margaret died. But, in some ways, she was amazed that Margaret made it that long, given all the close calls she'd had. Like the time she was fixing someone's barn, lost her balance and fell from the rafters. Brenda went to see her in the hospital in Pueblo, shocked to see her so banged up, broken and bruised.

But she'd been hurt many times, a fact that Brenda suspected had something to do with her I-can-do-it-myself attitude. A characteristic that few missed, even her obituary in the *Rocky Mountain News* read, "Ms. Locarnini believed in self-reliance to the end."[1]

Margaret's I-can-do-it attitude came into play when the two of them had planned to go to Mission: Wolf, the wolf preserve in Gardner. Margaret had somehow injured her right shoulder, but in true Margaret fashion, she was determined not only to go, but to drive. She insisted. So working the steering wheel and clutch, Margaret drove on, while Brenda, on cue, operated the stick shift. Reflecting on that day, Brenda told me, "That's how we spent the day in the car, me shifting and her doing the rest. It's who she was. She made a commitment, she followed through. She wasn't going to cancel the trip. We had to modify."

Brenda also knew Margaret had her demons. "She had deep, deep feelings and I think she, like a lot of us, had been hurt over and over and over through the years. I didn't know a lot about her family circumstances. She didn't talk about it much. She talked a lot about things she did rather than things she felt." She never talked about the losses in her life, about her heartbreak, and when her health began deteriorating, she avoided mentioning any pain she was having, although she'd go to bed early, or have a drink to dim the pain. But she would talk about a new way of carving wood, or an art project at school with which the kids had made noticeable progress and were excited, or the boy in the detention center she was tutoring on a volunteer basis.

Brenda watched how smart, agreeable Clara could be so amazingly patient with Margaret. She thought of Margaret as fire and Clara as water, calming Margaret down. But there were some difficult years, some times that were really hard for Margaret and therefore, hard on Clara. The last few, when Margaret suspected she had cancer but kept it to herself, were among them. It was a demon she thought she could fight first by ignoring it, then by sheer determination. But that wasn't possible in the end, and the struggle took its toll on both of them.

---

1 "Teacher, rancher Locarnini touched many lives," *Rocky Mountain News*, Denver, CO, Nov. 6, 2007, Obituaries.

Both with strong, independent spirits, Margaret and Clara ranked among the most generous people in the world in Brenda's eyes. She, as others did, admired how they helped people in need, and especially the kids they took in. She was glad that so many of them came back to the ranch as successful, happy adults wanting to see the people and place that had made such a difference in their lives.

There were many, and their stories varied, from teenage pregnancy, to abuse, to just needing an adult to talk with. Among them were Mike Haga, whose story I related earlier in "Haven;" the young woman who was now head of social services in Dubuque, Iowa; Corey Carey, now a teacher and counselor in Kenya, and his brother, Alex, who has a computer programming business in Mancos, Colorado; the phone call and follow-up email message from Bryan Christiansen, now chairman of a global business analytics and management consultancy. Having traveled the world, learned multiple languages, written articles and edited books,[2] Bryan was quick to give his English teacher, friend and mentor the credit she deserved. And of course, Clara was thrilled to hear from him.

It wasn't only that they'd helped so many kids that impressed Brenda. They also took care of Margaret's mother and aunt, moving them and their husbands into homes on the ranch, looking after Aunt Marg and her husband for thirty years, and Dorothy and Mike for some twenty-five. And it had been the end of their years, not always smooth going given the uneasy relationship between Margaret and her stepfather. Brenda thought there must have been a million examples of how they'd give of themselves or lent their horses, or whatever it took if somebody needed something.

Their horses. A whole lot of people braided into their lives because of their horses, horses who reflected who Clara and Margaret were, how they treated animals—and people. As in other matters, they stood by their word, just as Clara's father and grandfather had considered an agreement, a handshake, sacrosanct, as did Margaret's father, so

---

2 One of which is *Cultural Variations and Business Performance: Contemporary Globalism,* IGI Global, March, 2012. For more information, see bryanchristiansen01.wix.com/bc1960

they guaranteed their horses. They would buy one back if circumstances altered or if someone wasn't satisfied, a rare situation, but if it came up, they were right there. But they took care in the breeding, foaling, raising, and training, so dissatisfied customers were unusual.

They began the process by paying close attention to selecting parent horses for temperament, and they continued attending closely, ensuring the young ones were handled gently and with discipline, "like kids in a classroom," Clara once described.

In his book, *Horse: How the Horse Has Shaped Civilizations*, Edward Chamberlin writes "all good horse trainers have something in common: they watch. They pay attention. Good horse trainers make the horse do what they want by the quality of their attention."[3]

With both kids and horses, I can see Clara watching. I've witnessed the quality of her attention. That's how she builds trust, sets expectations and boundaries, and knows when to gently reinforce these when needed. She knows, through that careful watching, the appropriate time to introduce new learning, providing guidance throughout in a kind, firm, reassuring way. And I can see the young horses responding wonderfully to such treatment, just as her many students did. When Clara stopped training the colts and fillies, as far as breaking them to ride, she chose trainers who'd use a similar approach, those who knew the value of watching.

Given that people all over the country bought their horses, from Florida to California and places in between, their approach got high marks. Their horses made them proud, and in so many ways. Miracle Nellie Ruth's success in national distance competition, or Jukebox as a barrel racer, Bing as a world-class dressage performer with a youth rider, another as a jumper, and on and on. Amos Moses had even been on the cover of *Appaloosa Journal*.[4] Sometimes they'd almost bust their buttons when they'd hear about one of their horses.

Helen Royal and Bette Casapulla, who goes by the name B, came into

3 J. Edward Chamberlin. *Horse: How the Horse Has Shaped Civilizations*, New York: BlueBridge Books, 2006, 47.
4 June, 1999, Vol. 53, No.5

their lives through horses. Helen and B run a horse therapy program called *Take the Reins* in Summit County, about one hundred fifty miles north of Singing Acres. They work with children and adults who have problems ranging from substance abuse, domestic conflicts, life-changing illness, and more.

Helen, a therapist, has had horses in her life forever. So has B, who brings her far-reaching experience in horse behavior and animal husbandry to their program. Mental health groups and social services refer individuals to them, knowing that these two, a horse from their herd and the client, will work as a team.

One day in the spring of 2000, when Helen had gone to Glenwood Springs for her work with Community Mental Health Center, she stopped by the local tractor supply store. It was a favorite of hers and she liked to drop by whenever she was in town. It was there that she happened to see a flyer about a ten-month-old Appaloosa. His name was Royal Jerry, called RJ, and he was for sale. She knew she had no reason at all to be looking for a horse because she already had one. But thinking of the Appy she'd had growing up, she thought it would be fun to check this one out.

She'd already worked with B for a few years with the equine assistance psychotherapy program, at that time called *Reins of Change*, through the mental health center. She had a vision that it could be a great fit to take a young horse and train it through the program, having participants, who were mostly kids, be part of the process. They could see a horse grow up, learn about all the things a horse has to learn, and the horse could learn about working with different people.

With this vision and the memory of her own Appaloosa, Helen called Singing Acres Ranch and talked with Clara. Their horses, in demand for their quality and the ranch's strong reputation, went for fairly high prices. But when Clara found out about the idea for RJ to become a therapy horse, she instantly reduced his price, and by a significant amount. Delighted that Clara could share this vision for RJ, Helen was surprised by and grateful for Clara's generosity.

I remember being at the ranch a little while after Clara and Helen talked and how excited Clara and Margaret were about RJ's potential future. They'd seen countless instances of their horses helping young people recover from a trauma, or just grow up, and the idea that one of their horses would be specifically trained and positioned to help so many thrilled them. What could be better?

When Helen and B drove the hundred fifty miles to see RJ and meet Clara and Margaret, Helen's first impression and lasting memory was that of profound genuineness and acceptance. The feel of the solid, old house, the warmth of Margaret and Clara's reception, the beauty of the surrounding country. The connection among the four was instantaneous.

Helen and B were impressed by RJ right off the bat. Described by Clara as a "few spot Appy," with brown neck and shoulders fading into a white blanket, he was a beauty. This was as he should have been since Regals Royal sired him. To Clara, Regals Royal was the best stallion they'd ever had, given his confirmation, color— small spots, and temperament. And RJ inherited lots of his daddy's qualities.

B and Helen took RJ into the round pen and worked him before making the final decision. And before they did, Clara showed them another horse, a flashier one. In the end, they decided on RJ, a decision they've always been pleased with. So were Margaret and Clara, who would glow when they heard the stories from the program.

The stories also captivated me when Clara or Margaret shared a newspaper article, a letter, or told me the latest from a conversation with Helen or "B". I was intrigued about how the team used the natural being of the horse as an experiential way for clients to learn more about themselves. Helen explained how the horses give very immediate, honest feedback, and how they mirror what's going on for clients and usually offer a way for them to explore healthier ways of dealing with their issues.

In describing how it worked, Helen said that at the first session, they tell clients about each horse's personality and background. Then they give them a halter and tell them to go catch the horse they want to work with. The client goes out, B and Helen observe, then after the session, they talk through with the client how it went. How did the client deal with this task? Did he or she ask for help? Why? Why not? How did she feel? Helen and B offered their observations, too, to help the client look at his or her own behavior.

Their stories helped me understand just how powerful an experience this could be for someone stuck in a tough personal problem, whether triggered by a traumatic incident, a serious medical condition, or a deeply ingrained, counterproductive response to situations. One instance in which RJ played a role came about when he was barely two, not yet being ridden. The client was a young teen whose whole family had been in a car accident in which the father had been killed. This was horror enough, but as a middle child, she also had other issues. With an exceptionally intelligent older sister and a younger sister considered the baby, she struggled with where she stood in the family and how to be recognized as worthy in her own right. This in addition to, or perhaps heightened by, the tragedy her family had suffered.

The girl, whom I'll call Sally, wouldn't talk about what she wanted or needed, but she still expected, or at least fervently desired, that her mom know and respond accordingly. She didn't accept that her mom wouldn't automatically know what was so obvious to Sally. Her unexpressed, and therefore unmet, needs would build up to a boiling point and she'd explode. Lashing out at her mom, she'd get the same directed back at her. It was a tough situation for them both.

Sally was referred to *Take the Reins*. In the first session, after the horse introductions, B asked which one she wanted. Sally said, "Oh, RJ, because he's so cute!"

B wondered about her choice because despite being a wonderful horse, RJ showed a bit of that App stubbornness, and she'd made a point of talking about this when she'd introduced him. She knew that stubborn streak was there despite Singing Acres' breeding for disposition, and in B's mind, the lovely nature of their horses in general. But, knowing that many forces were in play, she and Helen went with Sally's choice, as they did with every client.

Out grazing in the pasture, RJ was intent on the lush grasses and not on much else when Sally picked up the halter and marched off toward the grazing horse, intent on catching him. Once in front of him, she stopped and looked at him, halter hanging in her hand. RJ grazed on.

B and Helen watched the scene before them. Horse and girl stood together in the pasture, RJ grazing, oblivious to Sally's wishes. Sally standing by him saying nothing, doing nothing, only looking at him. For the entire hour.

When the session ended, B and Helen held their usual debriefing. Upset by what had happened—or not happened—Sally immediately fired off, "Well! He didn't do what I wanted."

"How could he know what you wanted?" Helen asked.

"I was right there by him."

"But you didn't try to get his attention, you didn't try to get him to pick his head up so you could put the halter on," B observed.

"I was standing by him. He should have known."

"How could he know? Any of our five horses would've done the same thing. They're awesome, but they somehow have to know what you want. How do you think you might get them to know that?"

And so it went until Sally began to see that she had to do more than show up, that she had to know what she wanted and communicate it to RJ. Helen saw the look in her eyes when this realization dawned. It didn't take long for her to understand that expressing her needs applied to relationships with people, as well.

There were times, however, that RJ seemed to know exactly what was needed. The time a young man with multiple sclerosis and his girlfriend came to the program was one. The man, let's call him Sam, had been an extreme athlete, but then he suffered a sudden and aggressive onset of multiple sclerosis. Soon confined to a wheelchair, Sam found his sight going, as well. His girlfriend had unexpectedly become his caregiver. With the abrupt and dramatic shift in their relationship, they came to B and Helen for couple's therapy, seeking a way to understand their new situation, to learn how to accept and cope with their changing lives and altered roles.

Take the Reins had not yet had such a client, and the horses had never seen a wheelchair. But B and Helen felt complete trust in their horses, and they decided to see if they could help somehow.

Helen wheeled Sam into the inner corral, while the horses watched from a short distance away. She stopped and set the wheelchair's brakes, the horses continuing to watch. After a few minutes, they began to move. But rather than jostling for position to be the first and closest to check out the curious sight, as horses tend to do, they calmly ambled over to where he sat. As if planned, the horses formed a circle around Sam and stood quietly gazing at him.

Acting perhaps on some instinct, RJ stepped forward, strolled over and put his head down toward Sam's lap. Sam reached out and stroked the horse's head, murmuring something to him. After a few minutes, RJ sauntered away.

Each horse, one by one, approached Sam, put its head down to be petted, then moved away. Slack-jawed with shock, Helen and B extended the session, this lesson in acceptance. They'd never seen anything like it. B said thinking about this story still makes her cry. How could it not?

The horses were a high point in Sam's life, although the couple struggled to find answers through a number of activities in the program. They found no final or lasting one, but the connection with the horses proved a rare bright spot in daunting circumstances, a strand of goodness.

Around 2009, B and Helen learned about another SAR horse, Snowbird, often called Bird. He'd run into problems with its owners, and Clara, because of their guarantee, had bought him back from the man. Bird had served as a show horse for his daughters for a number of years, but then the girls either didn't want to or couldn't show him anymore.

The dad decided Bird needed a job, and the one available was as packhorse on a hunting trip. As an arena horse, a show horse, Bird had excelled. He'd been handled by the daughters, who'd doted on him. Now he was to experience something quite different, something that required unfamiliar equipment, travel over varying terrain, and unusual, inanimate cargo. The experience proved to be a damaging one. On the hunting trip, Bird fell off a ledge and was badly hurt.

When Clara heard about the incident, she was furious with the man for giving Bird a job for which he was so ill suited. She took the injured horse back and put him in pasture. She wanted to let him, in her words, "be a horse and relax for a couple of years," to fully recover from the ordeal. Whispers of coming and going.

Snowbird's accident didn't diminish his beauty. During his convalescence, artist Linda Gulinson photographed him, and from the photograph, painted a stunning picture. The painting, an impressive thirty inches by forty inches, now hangs in Clara's living room. Linda's specialty lay in Western art, with a focus on Native Americans, and more specifically, on Native American children. But when Singing Acres Ranch came into her life, she began to paint horses.

Linda and husband Jordan came across Singing Acres one day in the early 1990s. Driving from Westcliffe back to Denver, they saw Appaloosas out grazing. They thought the horses stunning, and the setting, a long, lush meadow complete with a pond smack-dab in the middle, seemed the perfect backdrop. They stopped to have a longer look, and then they drove on to the ranch house and into the yard to ask if they could take pictures.

Margaret was home at the time, and it was she who responded to the ruckus Opy and Whoopy made when the Gulinsons drove up. Those big, sleek Great Danes were the self-appointed canine welcoming party, and they took on the role with great enthusiasm.

When Margaret learned that the Gulinsons wanted photos for Linda to paint from, the artist in her responded with gusto. Of course, they could take as many pictures as they wanted, Margaret told them. And she proceeded to show them around the place, introducing them to the mares and foals then in the "condo," the special barn for expecting and new moms and their babies. Later, Linda and Jordan went back to the pasture where the grazing Apps had first caught their attention.

The couple visited the ranch numerous times over the years. Early in their friendship the ranch was dealing with the problem Susan's horse had introduced, the red scours described in Chapter 11. As a doctor, Jordan proved a valuable resource for Clara, who appreciated that he'd explain any drug she'd mention. He seemed to enjoy helping in that way, and Clara took full advantage of his expertise.

When the Gulinsons came to visit, Margaret and Clara would get the colts to do all kinds of exciting things for Linda's camera, run, frolic, chase each other. As a result, Singing Acres Ranch horses grace not only corrals and pastures across the country, but also the walls of many homes and offices through Linda's paintings.

Of the many Singing Acres paintings by Linda, two hold places of honor in the living room at the ranch. In one, three SAR horses, heads and necks pictured, are clustered together in such a way that suggests they're having a little confab. At the top is Matilda, then Sophie, and Sixteen Tons. Linda painted it early in the friendship and titled it "Gossip."

The other is the later one of Bird when he was convalescing, in which he's standing by the pond looking around to his left. His mahogany bay coloring is sprinkled with a few white App spots across his rump, his black mane and lower legs contrasting beautifully with his coat. He exudes tranquility.

A painting hangs across the room from Bird. This one by Charles A. Morris, not Linda, but because of its importance to Clara, I'd be remiss if I didn't include it. It's of Clara's beloved Queen, the horse on which she raced the Doodlebug, the horse she brought from Kansas, the horse that will always hold center place in her heart. I believe all her horses have places in her heart and she can cite mare and stallion from which each offspring came at the drop of a hat. The three horses in "Gossip" all came from Queen.

One day when Helen and B were at the ranch, they met Bird, and they fell in love right away. Given his calm disposition, Clara was sure he'd make a good therapy horse and sure enough, he was a hit in the program.

At first, although sweet and well mannered, he was a little standoffish, not connecting immediately. This wasn't a problem since Helen and B knew that their horses' quirks could also be assets for their clients. So when they did horse introductions, they told his story in terms of what clients themselves may have experienced. They talked about how Bird had overcome hardships himself, that he'd been hurt and was scared to connect.

B thought that whether this was true for a horse is anyone's guess. But the idea worked well for kids who needed to learn to overcome adversities themselves. It was especially useful for those who'd never been around horses to hear about Bird's reserve. Many people in the program hadn't had first-hand experience with horses, and it was Bird they instinctively trusted. Kids and adults gravitated to his calmness.

Once, when a newspaper reporter came to do a story on the program, B and Helen offered to take her through a traditional first session. As usual, they gave highlights of horses' stories that they thought most closely paralleled the client's story and let her take it from there.

This reporter had been in nursing but had recently changed her career to journalism. Although happy with the change, she knew that because she was new to the work, she hadn't yet developed much confidence in her ability to do it. She was right in the middle of the crossroads of rediscovering herself, with all its doubt and uncertainty. When she heard about how Bird had been a show horse, how he'd then been used as a packhorse and suffered the accident that triggered his return to Clara and subsequent move to *Take the Reins*, she chose him.

She could tell he was a little cautious, mirroring her own restraint, her own uncertainty. She had, in fact, been afraid to get close to a horse. They were new to her, and they were big. It took her some time to go near him, then longer to be able to touch him.

When the article appeared, Helen was pleased to see it written it as the reporter's own story, that what had happened between her and Bird was a fitting reflection of the program's power and effectiveness. In an accompanying photo, she had her arms around Bird's neck, hugging him.

Snowbird has a special place in my heart, too. On May 10, 1992, the first anniversary of my sister's death, David, my partner in life, and I were at Singing Acres. It had snowed the day before and the air held the memory of the storm, misty clouds cloaking the mountains and hanging low over the meadow. Inside having morning coffee with Margaret and Clara, I was soaking in the warmth of the fire from the old rock fireplace and the warmth of our friendship as we sat around catching up on what had been going on in our lives. David was out taking in the crisp morning air and enjoying poking around in the rustic mountain setting. Without warning, he burst through the door, breathless with excitement. "There's a baby, and it's just barely here!" he cried.

We jumped up and sprinted outside, behind the house and up to the corral by the "condo." Sure enough, there in a snow bank lay a beautiful bay foal, minutes old, his mother standing over him. She gave us only a brief look, as if to say, "Isn't he something?"

David and I watched the newborn struggle to his feet for the first time, his long, skinny black legs wobbling with the effort. A few minutes earlier, he'd been in a warm, dark place, now there was brightness, cool, soft air, and a whole world to become acquainted with.

Seeing this new life seemed such a gift, on that day of all days—a first anniversary I'd approached with apprehension—and he was a beauty. The day had turned into a beauty, too. The bright Colorado sun had burned off the misty clouds, revealing a brilliant sky, a smiling sky one could say. It was as if the sun were greeting the brand-new baby, too.

Soon after, back at home in Denver, we talked with Clara. "It seemed only natural to call him Snowbird," she told us. We agreed. It seemed the perfect name.

Having been there when Snowbird arrived, hearing the stories about him over time, listening to Brenda and so many others tell about Margaret and Clara, I think of the many ways our lives are braided, intertwined whether we're kin or not, whether we're horses or human. We touch each other's lives, often unexpectedly, catching up, blending in, letting go. This is the rhythm of the strands, the whispers of coming and going. This is the rhythm that spoke to me on the first anniversary of Susan's death, that spoke to my heart with the birth of that beautiful colt. And this is the rhythm of Singing Acres Ranch that speaks to me still.

13

No Regrets
1997 –

Frank Sinatra's voice crooned *My Way* in the recesses of my mind as I read Michelle Chapman's words in the transcript before me. "I don't think Margaret had any regrets," Michelle had said. "She told Kevin and me about different guys she'd dated, but I don't think she had any regrets about not marrying. I think she would've liked to have had children, but she felt fulfilled by the kids they helped and adopted."

Michelle continued as, thankfully, Frank took a break, "And she got to travel. Hawaii for work on her Master's Degree, China, Alaska, and points in between."

Michelle and I had talked by phone the week before, but now that I was looking at her words again, I was struck by the word "regrets." What a powerful force it can be in our lives. Many of us work hard not to have regrets, or we deny them in case they imply we've failed somehow, or we learn from them as we carry on. Or perhaps we live our lives in such a way they're neither here nor there, they're inconsequential in the big picture.

Intrigued, I began poking around the Internet to see what was out there on the topic. An article from *Forbes Magazine* entitled "The 25 Biggest Regrets in Life. What Are Yours?"[1] caught my attention. I read it with Margaret and Clara in mind. Many regrets the author Jackson listed had to do with being too busy to pay attention to family and friends, or living the life your parents wanted you to live rather than the one you wanted. A related one was not applying for your dream job. And of course, worrying about what others think of you. As I read the list, thinking of those two, I found myself saying, "Nope, nope, nope,

---

1 Eric Jackson, (*www.forbes.com/sites/ericjackson*), 10/18/2012

not this one either."

One about not taking life so seriously, about not joking around or having fun got a resounding "Nope!"

After more perusing of books, online offerings, and words by Montaigne, Swami Sivananda, Nathan Hale and others, I came across something British actor Basil Rathbone, of Sherlock Holmes and Robin Hood fame, said that stopped me in my tracks. It seemed to fit for both Margret and Clara. Mr. Rathbone said, "Never regret anything you have done with sincere affections, nothing is lost that is born of the heart."[2]

"Born of the heart." Everyone I'd talked with, everyone I knew who knew those two spoke of their honesty and open-heartedness, their generosity and caring for others, for the land, for the life they led. How could they have many regrets? "Sincere affection" imbued their lives.

And Lucille Ball had something to say that took me right back to Clara's classroom in Kingman, Kansas. Ms. Ball said, "I'd rather regret the things I've done than the things I haven't done."

This kind of thinking had propelled Clara and Margaret into action, into looking for that ranch in Colorado, into following that path to their dream.

Michelle went on to say, "I think we were just another two kids to them, the last of them. I look back and Margaret's death was, to me, kind of like a mother dying, a second one. I really thought of her as a mother—an ornery one."

Kids and comrades surrounded Margaret and Clara, forming the Singing Acres de facto family, becoming part of it in various ways. Michelle and husband Kevin met Margaret and Clara during a major snowstorm in 1997. It was the granddaddy blizzard that helped clinch the decision for Mike Haga and David Brothers to move from Custer County to Grand Junction. But Michelle and Kevin had the reverse intention. They wanted to buy a house in the area, and they'd just looked at one near Singing Acres Ranch.

Driving back through the blowing snow on icy Highway 96 from

---

2 *http://www.brainyquote.com/quotes/keywords/regret.html*

Westcliffe, they spotted horses out on the road. Their concern for the horses and other drivers told them to do something. Stopping at the first house they came to, they knocked on the door. It turned out the house was Margaret's and Clara's, but the horses weren't. After brief introductions and the couple's explanation of the problem, the ranchers went out and got the horses in anyway, herding them into one of their corrals in the midst of the raging storm, impressing the young couple.

Not long after, the Chapmans, despite their low bid on the house they'd looked at that day, ended up buying it. Michelle attributed their luck in getting it to their being the only ones who could make it up its steep driveway in all kinds of weather. The driveway is, indeed, steep. They became neighbors to Singing Acres Ranch, which was lucky again for them, and lucky for Margaret and Clara. The four came to care for each other and knew they could call upon the other for whatever was needed. And some of the calls were for more than the can-I-borrow-a-wrench variety.

Kevin often helped out with a difficult foaling. If the colts didn't handle well, he was the one Clara put in charge of holding them after they were born. He knew horses, and he was gentle and steady. He re assured them. Kevin was also the one Clara called when the vet couldn't make it to the ranch and a horse had to be put down. She knew he'd do what needed to be done and in the best way he could, quickly and with care.

Kevin and Margaret became regular hunting buddies, and Michelle learned to cut up the meat. She told me about a time when they'd spent a whole weekend butchering an elk Kevin had shot. A day or two later when they went to get some from the freezer, it was gone. They couldn't find even a small package. They asked Margaret if she knew what had happened to it.

"Aww. Just shut up, you two," she grumbled. "You didn't need it anyway."

The couple soon learned there was a local family who did need it, and Margaret had given all of it to them. Admitting this was exactly what had happened, she granted, "Okay, you can raid my freezer if you need to."

Margaret's friends knew what a joker and teaser she was, and some of them had fun teasing her back. Michelle clearly remembered the night they came up with "Margaret's Rules of Hunting." Kevin and Clara threw out one rule after another, all drawn from Margaret's adventures, misadventures, and her own quips about them. The more they volleyed the one-liners back and forth, the more peeved Margaret became. Michelle found the whole scene hilarious, Clara and Kevin playing off one another, Margaret stomping around, huffing and puffing.

"Wrecking a car filled with bread and vegetables in a pasture is not bear baiting."

"The best time to poach is in hunting season."

"Don't use a Great Dane to find downed game."

And the infamous, "Don't worry; I know right where it is. You can drive right to it. I can walk to it."

"Famous last words:

'That's not a big rock!'
'That's not a deep hole.'
'That's an anthill, not a tree stump.'
'Do not sight in your gun on an antelope.'[3]
'The snow isn't deep.'
'Four-wheel drive will go anywhere.'"

Famous last words, my monkey's uncle. Margaret stomped off. The remaining three laughed until they could barely draw breath.

Michelle often went fishing with Margaret. That was the way it was with those two. From the time they met, Margaret took Michelle on adventures. Often without warning, she'd show up in the morning, like the spring day they went to the dairy in Florence. It was fairly soon after a number of calves had been born, and Margaret was looking for the males, which the dairy didn't keep. She found three that she liked

3 I had to ask my hunter brother, Bruce, about this one. He said you have to sight in your gun, that is, align the scope with where the bullet will go, before you go hunting. Game are too fast to do it when you're getting ready to shoot.

and loaded them into the back of her Toyota station wagon. She told Michelle to make them stay put. Michelle found herself sitting in the back, coaxing and reassuring the calves the whole way back up to the ranch. "Sit, down, stay, sit down, stay, stay ... " She'd never talked to calves before.

On another outing, Margaret stopped for Michelle and another neighbor, telling them they were going fishing. Margaret drove them south to Rye, about forty-five minutes away, where she pulled into a privately-owned pasture.

Michelle asked if Margaret knew those people.

"Oh, sure, sure," Margaret said, then added, "but let's hide the truck behind the trees, anyway."

Enjoying the outings and their time together, they developed a trust that allowed Margaret to talk about things she rarely discussed with others. Knowing Margaret's devotion to her Aunt Marg, the aunt who'd always been close, the aunt she'd moved to Colorado and whom she'd cared for to the end of her life, Michelle also knew Aunt Marg's death came as a tremendous blow. Michelle recalled when it happened back in 2004 and how Margaret went into a kind of frenzy. She didn't sleep for days, and Clara had become concerned about her. Clara called Michelle for help, asking for something she knew Margaret would agree to. "Will you take Margaret fishing?"

Of course Michelle was happy to do anything.

The wintry day seemed to fit the quiet mood inside the car as the two drove the thirty minutes to Lake DeWeese on their ice-fishing mission. Soon after they arrived, they found an abandoned hole someone had chopped in the ice, so they cleared the slush from it and threw their hooks in. Then they settled in to wait for the fish.

But Margaret didn't settle in very well. She began pacing, and Michelle watched as she walked around and around. Margaret couldn't be still, she seemed compelled to keep moving, round and round the fishing hole. Michelle wouldn't soon forget how Margaret talked steadily that day, apparently needing to go through all that was on her mind, while Michelle nodded encouragement and uttered sympathetic words.

They spoke of death, Margaret telling Michelle about her sister, Louise, about her own fear of death, about all the losses she'd had, about all the things that were bothering her. She talked and walked and walked and talked. Finally, she lay down on the ice and fell asleep. Michelle watched her sleep soundly, deeply, for hours, right there on the ice. When she awoke, Michelle thought it was as if some kind of reset button had been pushed. Margaret was back to herself, no longer frenzied, no longer compelled to pace.

It was this incident that impressed on Michelle just how afraid of death her friend was. After that, the two had quite a few conversations about it. And about cancer, which, in itself, terrified Margaret.

In retrospect, Michelle could see signs of a problem. Margaret wasn't eating much of anything, and she'd get extremely tired. Many early evenings when Michelle and Kevin dropped by, Margaret would already be asleep. Putting it all together afterwards, she regretted not having comprehended the situation. She wished she'd seen these signs for what they were at the time and pressed Margaret to consult a doctor. At the same time, Michelle knew you just didn't press Margaret about anything. Even well-intentioned, being pressed wasn't something Margaret responded to favorably. Her friends knew it would only make her less likely to do whatever she was being urged to do.

That Margaret and Clara were such complete opposites, in Michelle's mind, made them a unique team. Clara seemed quieter, although also a laugher who enjoyed jokes and pranks. But she seemed to prefer being in the background. "She was supportive, like, if we were cutting up meat, Clara would be the one who sharpened the knives," Michelle told me.

And while Clara grew up on a farm and Margaret had been more of a city girl, Clara seemed disinterested in hunting and not likely to slaughter animals for food. Michelle loved the story Clara told about how, when she was on the farm in Kansas, the family were going to raise bunnies for the meat. But none of them could kill any of the bunnies, and they had hundreds of them.

"So what did you do with them?" Michelle wanted to know.

"We let them loose. The farmers didn't like us much, but we couldn't kill them," Clara explained.

A heart of gold, Michelle thought, and she was in good and plenteous company with that assessment. That company included Mildred Halle for one. Mildred lived about eight miles back in the mountains behind Singing Acres Ranch. Before Margaret died, Mildred didn't know Clara all that well, because Clara didn't talk much when she was around. Mildred and Margaret did all the talking and, I suspect, just as Michelle said, Clara stayed in the background. But after Margaret was gone, Mildred and Clara talked every day, often multiple times. And she kept Clara well supplied with homemade cookies, pies, bread and all kinds of other treats. Mildred's heart had some of that gold in it, too.

Mildred came onto the scene through Caroline Shellenberger, a mutual friend. From Wisconsin, she was looking for land in the area. Once when we talked, Mildred told me she couldn't remember a whole lot about when she first met Clara and Margaret because she was so jealous, wishing she'd be born and raised here, wishing she could've had a ranch like Singing Acres. That was *her* big regret.

Then after she bought a place and moved to Custer County in 1996, Margaret and Clara helped her out in many ways, including getting firewood from their land. They also aided in getting a Christmas tree every year, that is, Margaret did. Clara went with her once and the tree Mildred picked was huge. She'd always wanted a gigantic tree that would hit the ceiling, and this one would do that. It was a whopper. In Mildred's words, "We damn near killed ourselves lifting it."

Clara confirmed Mildred's assessment, noting that Mildred hadn't had experience moving trees, so she didn't know about the role of balance in doing it. But they got it into the back of good old Bertha, the trusty 1973 four-wheel-drive Ford pickup, then to Mildred's house and into her living room.

Clara told her she never was going with her again, and she didn't. But their friendship grew anyway, and Mildred couldn't imagine not having Clara in her life. She admired what Clara and Margaret had done at Singing Acres, even if she didn't get to do the same herself.

As for Bertha, in 2006, Margaret and Clara gave her to David and me to use at Stillpoint. She served us well for years thereafter, as she'd served Margaret and Clara for the thirty-three years they had her.

In 1997, Virginia Moraga moved into the old school house down the road from Singing Acres, the same schoolhouse Sherry Campbell lived in when she first came to the area. Virginia went over to the ranch and introduced herself, and right off the bat yet another friendship began.

Virginia held close her memories of getting up early in the morning to have coffee with Clara and Margaret. This was a cherished ritual she'd had with her grandmother, who'd passed seventeen years earlier. Virginia told me, "It wasn't that they reminded me of my grandmother, but that ritual reminded me of being home."

She said that both Clara and Margaret became her compass as she ventured though having her knee replaced, losing her job with the Bureau of Prisons, and getting through a broken relationship. In Virginia's words, "Neither judged me for my poor decisions but were supportive despite them."

Seeing Clara as the stabilizing force in the relationship, Virginia called herself and Margaret partners in crime, teasing, joking, and getting into mischief. Clara described the two as being joined at the shoulder, they were so *compatico.* Even so, to Virginia, Margaret's sense of humor could sometimes be a little warped. She could see that if Margaret knew she could intimidate you, that would open the door to having fun with you. Kind of like a cat and mouse game.

If you got to know Margaret, you got to know she liked to make up words to suit particular situations. Virginia chuckled when she recalled Margaret calling herself a Wapaho, priding herself on being part Italian. She had business cards made to support this notion, and wore a t-shirt proclaiming something about how Italians knew how to get rid of bodies.

When Virginia had to have a Dalmatian who was a fear-biter put down, Margaret did it. She hid the body, refusing to tell Virginia where it was. When the person whose property it was on found the body, Virginia joked with Margaret, doubting that she really could be part Italian, having failed in body disposal. Familiar with being stereotyped regarding gender and ethnicity, Virginia could laugh at its absurd side, too.

It was rare for Margaret and Clara to be the targets of crime of any sort, but it did happen. Once, in the middle of the night, two prisoners who'd escaped from the county jail in Westcliffe crept into the yard and stole Margaret's Toyota. A few days later, the police found it in Denver. As Virginia remembered it, unbeknownst to the prisoners or the cops, Margaret kept the ashes of a close friend on the floor of the back seat. After the police returned the car, she said, "It's about time my friend got out for a drive."

Eventually, the police caught the escapees and took them back to Westcliffe. Virginia, who was then a detention officer, along with a deputy were detailed to take one of them to court in Canon City. On the way, they decided to stop for a quick lunch at Quiznos, but neither had any money. Virginia called Margaret and asked if she could lend them some for lunch. Margaret agreed, and when they got to Singing Acres, they parked across the highway and Virginia ran to the house to get the cash.

Arriving there, she saw that Margaret, Clara, and Sandy were trying to move a love seat out through the door. Margaret asked, "Can you help us move this thing, Virginia?"

"Sorry," Virginia replied. "We have the guy who stole your Toyota in the van, and we need to get him over to Canon."

Margaret stood up straight, turned around, grabbed her rifle from the nearby case, and said, "I want to have a few words with him."

"You can't do that, Margaret," Virginia said, breathing a sigh of relief that the love seat filled the doorway preventing Margaret from getting out.

But, to illustrate Margaret's multi-faceted nature, Virginia related how Margaret later worked with another inmate to help him get his GED, no rifle involved.

If Margaret was Virginia's partner in crime, then Clara was Virginia's confidant. Not quick to act, in Virginia's eyes, Clara's methodical weighing of possibilities, pros and cons, invited trust. And the fact that her friend also enjoyed practical jokes made it all that much better.

One time they were at the winter corral checking on Clara's horse Romeo, and someone stopped by and asked about the horse. Virginia told him his name was *Romero* and that he was a rare Mexican Quarter Horse. Clara, in earshot of the conversation, burst into her exuberant whole-hearted laugh when she heard the visitor's response indicating he believed it. After that, when some unsuspecting person asked Clara about the horse, she used Virginia's line to describe him, laughing to herself every time.

Most importantly to Virginia, when in 2001 she introduced Kristi Jo, her new partner, to Margaret and Clara, they welcomed her in. Virginia told me the thing that doubly clinched the friendship with Margaret was when Margaret told Kris, "If you can cook, she will love you forever."

Kris responded, "She already does," and that was the start of another friendship.

The friendship with Kris, a nurse, grew over the next six years, and when Margaret went home from Hospice, Kris became part of her health-care team. She was assisting on the first day of deer season when she heard Margaret say to Clara, "I don't know why, but I have to do this."

"This" meant go out to hunt, to try to get a deer. It *was* the first day of hunting season, after all. She was too weak even to lift a gun, but Kris helped her into the Toyota and they drove where they could, through the pasture, at the edge of aspen and spruce stands, talking and scouting as they rode. It was a chance for Margaret to tell Kris of her years of hunting, of her joy in being out with her wonderful hunting partners, especially Danny. Although they didn't see a deer that day, Kris believed Margaret relished the time they were out and savored sharing her memories while looking for deer.

Bringing to mind how, a few days later one of those favored hunting partners, Jimmy Sewell, had taken Margaret hunting again, Kris said she was very glad Margaret got her last deer. That Jimmy had had to help her hold the rifle, showed just how much it meant to Margaret to have that final hunting experience.

When Virginia and Kris learned about Margaret's cancer, they were both devastated. Virginia told me she cried like she'd never cried before. While Margaret was in Hospice, Virginia went to see her, lying down by her and taking a nap with her. When she had to leave, she asked Margaret, "When you get to the other side, will you give me a message that everything is alright?"

Margaret said she would. A while later, several unusual things happened, reminding Virginia of this exchange. As she related to me, "Some time after she passed, Kris and I were heading home. We had just turned on to Oak Creek Grade and I turned the radio off. Right before I pulled on our driveway, the radio turned on. Kris and I looked at each other, and then I remembered what I asked of Margaret."

There was more. Virginia said, "To this day when I am driving a bit too fast, a deer or some animal will run in front of me, and I will laugh and say, 'Okay, Margaret, I'll slow down.' Sometimes the cat will go after things in the air, and I will say, 'Margaret, leave the cat alone,' and the cat will stop."

In December of 2008, Virginia graduated from the Police Academy. While Virginia was saddened that Margaret wasn't there to see that day, she was thrilled that a proud Clara was.

Around 2012 circumstances caused Virginia and Kris to decide to move to South Dakota, near Kris's family. It was a tough decision. But Kris had been hired by the VA hospital at Fort Meade and moved to Spearfish in August while Virginia stayed in Westcliffe to start packing their three bedroom home—singlehandedly. In October, Kris found a house in Spearfish and then returned to Colorado to make the big move. With the help of friends from the American Legion, Virginia and Kris loaded up a twenty-four-foot truck, a twenty-foot truck, Virginia's truck, their Suzuki, Kris's sister and sister-in-law, four dogs, and six cats and drove on to settle in Spearfish.

The two women came back to see Clara once or twice a year, and they called often. Still, they missed her. Virginia's poignant comment made me realize how much. She said, "I hated to leave Clara and I miss her so. She is my family and Singing Acres is my home and refuge."

It's not surprising that Singing Acres is a refuge for many. Pat Schulze, the friend who was involved with Clara and Margaret in the libel court case,[4] had known them since she moved to Custer County some thirty-six years ago. She told me a heartwarming story about her situation after she moved to the area and Clara and Margaret's response to it.

Going through a tough transition, Pat was working four jobs to stay financially afloat. One day she stopped by the ranch for a short visit between jobs. The ranchers knew her situation and could see what it was doing to her. She'd known from the time she'd first met them they were kind people. But she was deeply touched when they told her, "Pat, if you ever need money, or you need anything, we have this can with money in it for our friends. If you ever need it, you're more than welcome to come get it."

Showing her where the can was, they said, "If we're not home, just come on in anyway and get what you need."

Pat told me she never needed money from that can, then asked, "How many people do you know who would tell you there's a can of money in their house and that, if you need anything, come in and get it?"

Pat had been talking to Clara earlier in the day that we talked. She asked Clara if she still had that can of money. Clara said, "Yeah. But I don't have it where I used to on the stairs because Corn Dog [the cat] has learned if he dumps the can over, some change will come out for him to play with. Now it's on top of that fridge. But I still have the can of money."

Tom, who's married to Pat, has known Clara and Margaret since the two women first moved there in 1965. His parents, Myrtle and Les, were good friends with them back when his folks ran cattle up on the national forest land. Les and Myrtle took Margaret and Clara under their wing,

---

4 See Chapter Eleven, "Sisters & Friends."

and showed them much of the country. Tom was the one who taught Margaret how to hunt antelope.

About every two weeks the Schulz family would have to move their cattle around to different pastures, and Margaret and Clara would help out. In Tom's words, "God knows, doing that kind of work you always need an extra hand. And those two knew what they were doing."

Given all the ventures Clara and Margaret had going, they needed extra hands, too. Tom's sister Claricy was the first to work for them. "Later, when they were running the riding camps, they always had horses that needed to be broke and trained, so my brother and I would break their horses for them," Tom told me.

Many years later, when Pat came into the picture, she broke and trained horses for Singing Acres, too. In fact, she trained my Arabian mare, Sara, an earlier offspring of the ill-fated Farasaya, the horse that brought my sister into Clara and Margaret's lives. And, in some kind of cosmic symmetry, Sara spent several years with Margaret and Clara, and the last years of her life at Pat and Tom's place. There, she was under the care of their granddaughter Jordan, who was four years old when she started riding Sara.

Pat and Tom both talked about what a highly respected teacher Clara was. Pat always admonished her that she couldn't retire till her kids were through school. Clara did retire a few years before Pat's son, Mark, graduated, but she still made quite an impression on him. In later years he liked to stop by the ranch with his son for a visit as often as he could. And Pat's daughter, Lisa, became a teacher. Pat attributed her choosing that profession to her good teachers, Clara being the central one.

With so many people declaring their esteem and affection for these two, I was curious about Clara's feelings about regret. When I talked with her, she said her only noticeable one was not living closer to her younger brother Ray so she could've spent more time with him. She acknowledged she'd made some mistakes, but she also accepted that she'd made her decisions as best she could, and she had no problem living with them. The main good decision being living her life at Singing Acres.

Ruminating on how Clara and Margaret lived the way they wanted to, my mind drifted to others who'd elected life on their own terms, especially to those who wrote about their own personal quests. Just the titles of these books I've read reveal plenty, enough to suggest they lived lives of choice, fueled by unflinching self-awareness and courage. Diverse people, all of them, all on diverse paths—explorers, spiritual teachers, and psychoanalysts among them.

One of the last great British explorers, Wilfred Thesiger, grew up in Abyssinia, now Ethiopia, a place that implanted in him "a life-long craving for adventures among untamed tribes in unknown lands."[5] He titled his autobiography *The Life of My Choice.*

Alan Watts, an unorthodox and wildly popular philosopher and cultural icon of the 1960s and 1970s, called his *In My Own Way.*[6] Marion Milner examined her life to learn what made her happy and what general principles underlay "conditions under which happiness occurred" and wrote about it in *A Life of One's Own.*[7]

Challenges and difficulties certainly play a role in these accounts. But regret seems to be missing, while satisfaction in following one's heart shines through.

Basil Rathbone's observation about sincere affection and doing things born of the heart does seem an antidote to regret. And to paraphrase Frank Sinatra, for Margaret and Clara, any regrets left are hardly worth mentioning.

5 Wilfred Thesiger. *The Life of My Choice.* London: Flamingo,1992, 442.
6 New York: Vintage Books, 1973.
7 Republished, Routledge, 2011. First published in 1934.

14

Being of Use
1991-

MELANIE CAMPER, NOW MELANIE CAMPER FALL, THE ALMOST eight-year-old kid who first encountered Margaret and Clara as they painted a storefront window for the Stampede all those years ago, came back into their lives in the early 1990s. At first, she saw them infrequently, maybe bumping into her former teachers in town.

On the occasion of Clara's retirement party in 1991, Melanie and some friends who had all been Clara's students were nearby, helping the Saddle Club with its Westcliffe Stampede gymkhana series. The series involved timed and judged competitions for kids and their horses. During a lull in the barrel racing, pole bending and other events, they slipped over to the celebration to give Miss Reida a hug and wish her well. She was, after all, their favorite teacher through all those school years and her retirement was a big deal in the school and community. Melanie noted the long list of names in the guest book as people came and went, the crowd ever changing, but never seeming to dwindle.

After Melanie left her work at the extension office for a job at the courthouse, she saw them more often. Car licensing, home and land titles for Margaret's aunt and mother and their husbands and the like brought them into the court house and into more frequent contact with Melanie.

In 1993, when Melanie and her husband, Scott, bought the old Otto Stein place a ways up behind Singing Acres, they became neighbors. The road to the Fall's place lies about half a mile west of Singing Acres' ranch house, running right by where Margaret's mom and aunt lived, across from one of the SAR corrals and barns.

That's where Margaret and Clara were feeding some of the horses one morning as Melanie drove by. She stopped to say hello and get a hug.

"We're sure glad to know you guys are back there," Clara said. "If you ever need anything let us know."

"I know you mean that," Melanie returned, "but I'm not going to be one of those neighbors who'll bug you all the time. Plus, I know you like your independence yourselves."

Melanie did like her independence, just as she liked being a good neighbor who would help out when needed, and stay out of the way when not. During her first years on the Stein place, Melanie spent much of her time at home caring for her youngest son, Casey, who was recovering from a corral accident he'd had when he was a toddler. Her older sons, Grady and Tanner Camper, both in school, also gave younger Casey lots of attention and support. As a family, they had plenty to do taking care of things at home.

Over time, as Casey improved, Clara and Margaret hired Melanie for various projects. Working at Singing Acres Ranch had been Melanie's long-time dream, and though it was only on special projects, she was doing just that.

She still felt a bit intimidated by Margaret, and not a little in awe of Clara. She cared deeply about both of them, and she found her care and respect coming out in different ways. It took years before she could smoke in front of Miss Reida, despite the fact that Miss Reida herself smoked, or to call her Clara. And she knew better than to suggest that Miss Locarnini not do something or do it a different way.

At the same time she knew she'd come far in understanding these two, far from the kid Miss Reida had startled by stopping her when she and her friend Idell were running their horses too hard. And far from the girl gagging on the tapioca pudding Miss Locarnini had made her eat—and which she threw up. Now she worked for and alongside both of these women, and she relished being part of the ranch's activities.

Thinking about Melanie's commitment to the ranch and to Margaret and Clara takes me back to Aristotle and his three motives for friendship[1]— usefulness, pleasure and being alike in excellence and virtue. As with many of the two ranchers' friendships, theirs with Melanie exemplified all three motives working together. Melanie wanted to be of use, she wanted to help these two women she admired so much, and they needed and appreciated her help. A delight to be with, Melanie venerated the land, the animals, and a sense of connection and community, as did Margaret and Clara.

Their shared stories, beginning the summer of 1966, reflected the friendship, which deepened over time. Then in 2007 when Melanie started working for them, new stories developed. The stories mattered to Melanie, just as being there, working on that ranch, being able to help mattered. Looking back, she could see that the stories that had etched themselves into her memory offered a trail into her understanding of the two friends. Stories that still made her laugh to the more serious that caused her to think about more weighty aspects of friendship.

One came from the time Melanie and her younger brother, Scotty, were out repairing and replacing Singing Acres fences and had followed the fence line to a particularly secluded gully. The old fence was fastened to tires filled with rocks and dirt so the animals couldn't go under it, a common practice in earlier days.

Getting the tires and throwing them out so they could haul them away was demanding work, but they went at it just as they did everything, with vigor and determination. Melanie remembers Scotty, hard at it with shovel and brute force, looking up at her and saying, "I'm pretty sure I found where Margaret hides the bodies."

That made Melanie bubble with laughter, thinking about how Margaret, who intimidated her still, was always telling her there probably were some bodies out there. Even as an adult, Melanie couldn't always be sure if her former nemesis was kidding or not.

Later, on the same fence job, Melanie was riding along when she saw a foot sticking out of a mine hole. All she could think was, "Holy shit! I did find where she hid the bodies!"

---

1 See Chapter Six, "A Community of Friends."

Staring at the foot, Melanie felt the slow dawn of realization. It wasn't a foot, it was a prosthesis. And there were several. When Melanie told her about the discovery, Clara got her turn for a big belly laugh. As soon as she could catch her breath enough to speak, she told Melanie the prostheses had belonged to Aunt Marg's husband, Darrell. After Darrel died, Margaret rounded up all of his prostheses, which he hadn't been able or willing to dispose of, and threw them down the mine hole. Some of them apparently didn't make their way down. No bodies, only wayward man-made limbs.

Noticing that Margaret and Clara were asking her to do more around the ranch, she thought it was likely linked to Margaret's not feeling well, and to some of the health problems Clara was dealing with too—shoulder, knee and respiratory issues.

In the spring of 2007, Margaret asked Melanie if she would fix some fences and set up some stock panels up. Melanie was working on the half-mile section between the ranch house and the guest house, formerly Aunt Marg's home, when she saw Margaret's old gray Toyota wagon coming down the road. The little white flag with its black skull and crossbones waved maniacally from the car's antenna, and dust clouds followed closely on the car's tail. Margaret.

"What are you doing? Ready for a break?" Margaret called from the car. "Come on up to the guest house"

"Well. I gotta … ," Melanie started, but Margaret cut her off.

"Just come on!"

So off she went to the guest house figuring Margaret wanted someone to hang out with. They'd work on puzzles, she figured, shoot the breeze and have a little wine, although Melanie wasn't much of a drinker. Still, she'd sip some to keep Margaret company.

One time when they were working on a puzzle, they heard sounds from the porch. They went to investigate and found Melanie's Great Pyrenees, Toodles, sitting there, shaking all over. Melanie noticed the sky was clouding up and thunder rumbled in the distance and figured that had terrified the dog so he'd gone to find his safety net, Melanie.

"Margaret, I need to get going and get Toodles home. He's scared to death. He'll just follow the truck back," Melanie told her.

But Margaret had a different idea. "Oh, no, no. I'll take him," she said.

"He doesn't get in vehicles."

"Oh, he'll get in," Margaret said as she opened the back of her Toyota and began pushing and shoving the massive animal into it.

All Melanie could see in the small car was Toodle's white fur, so completely had he filled the space. When they got to the house, about a half-mile away, Margaret backed the car, Melanie thought, as if she had a horse to unload at the front door. Opening the car's back door, Margaret commanded, "Okay Toodles, get out of there!"

Melanie saw the dog having a hard time moving and pointed it out. "Margaret, I think something's stopping him."

"Oh, no, he can go" Margaret insisted, continuing to urge the creature to get out.

Finally, Toodles did go, dragging the contents of Margaret's car, all affixed to his thick, long coat, with him. A fishing rod, tackle and yards of fishing line trailed behind the giant dog.

"Oh, Margaret!" Melanie exhaled.

Margaret assured her, "It'll be okay."

"But, I've got to get the hooks out of him!"

It took some time and cutting of hair to separate equipment from pooch, but they did what they could, removing a great many hooks. The critter's thick fur was pocked with holes by the time they finished, looking a bit as though moths had gotten to him. They put Margaret's stuff back in the car so she would have it in case she had a sudden urge to fish. But Melanie and Scott came across fish hooks in poor Toodle's heavy coat for months, reminders of Margaret's resolve, which some might call intractability, after-effects be damned.

Of the many stories Melanie shared with me, one that underlined aspects of nature we humans find difficult stood out. A series of events, it started on the last day of July, 2007. Melanie remembered it clearly.

She was having coffee on the deck when she looked over across the way at her horses. She thought, "They're lying in weird positions. Horses don't lie like that."

She put her boots on and walked across the meadow. As she got closer, she could tell both horses were dead. Seeing the terrible evidence before her, the blackened tree, the dead birds in it, led her to realize that her horses had been hit by lightning. There had been a severe storm the night before, so she figured they'd run to the tree for shelter. Then lightning hit, killing them instantly. There'd been no thrashing, no marks indicating they'd moved at all after the lightning struck.

Besides the grief of losing her horses, Melanie had to deal with what to do with them. She later told me, "One dead horse is major. Two dead horses … you don't know how much earth you got to dig up."

Since she and Scotty were working on the SAR fences, Melanie thought it would be okay to call Margaret and Clara and ask to borrow their back hoe and dump truck and haul the bodies up toward the top of the old ski area. She knew that was where they put their dead horses. "Of course," they said.

Thinking of this brought to my mind sky burial, a custom in Tibet and a few Chinese provinces. In earlier times, some Native Americans practiced sky burial. Many of these traditions believe that since life has left the body and only an empty shell remains, that shell can feed scavenging animals or decompose in a natural way on its own. Because the body is simply flesh and it has to be disposed of, doing so in the most generous way possible matters. Some place the bodies on mountaintops, others on rock structures. For some, the practice clearly demonstrates the impermanent nature of all things.

There was also the practical matter Melanie was concerned about— the actual burial. For two horses, that's a big hole. For people living in hard, rocky terrain, digging holes presents a problem, as does building fires for cremation in areas where trees are scarce.

I doubt that Melanie thought of a sky burial, but if she had, it might have helped prepare her for what happened next.

Margaret called Melanie about a week later. "If you had a chance to see a whole bunch of bears, would you want to see them?"

"Yes," Melanie said.

"Would you want to see them if they're eating your horses?"

Melanie thought for a minute about that question, then answered yes.

A few minutes later she and her son Casey were on their way to pick up Margaret. Melanie could see that Margaret hadn't been doing well recently, and the heart monitor she was wearing hinted at the search for the source of the problem. She didn't want Margaret crawling in and out of the back of the Bronco, so she told Casey to get in the back and Margaret could sit up front.

They drove up the bumpy trail to the spot Margaret had in mind, knowing they'd have to look fast since bears are shy and those around that area certainly weren't accustomed to people. But, Melanie thought, when dumpsters were involved, bears were not as easily startled by humans, since the presence of dumpsters meant human presence. But they were a long way from any dumpsters. As they approached the site, they saw the bears. Seven of them, all colors and sizes—darker, lighter, cinnamon. Intent on their feast, they took a moment to register human presence. But only a moment, and then they scampered off.

To Melanie's way of thinking, even that brief moment had been worth the effort, which included separating the thought of her horses from the scene of those bears before her.

"Let's drive up to the southwest top corner of the property." Margaret suggested, "Maybe we'll catch them coming through to circle back here."

They jumped back in the Bronco and headed upslope. A big rock Melanie had previously cleared in her little Bronco sat at the top of the trail. But Margaret didn't realize the car would clear, and before Melanie understood why, Margaret yelled at her to stop. Slamming on the brakes she watched Margaret jump out and start jostling the rock. An amazed Melanie saw her move it, while also seeing the toll it took on her to do so. Her face grew paler, her eyes squinted as if in reaction to pain, and her breath came in gasps.

Melanie was upset. She thought Margaret could've told them what she intended, then big, strong Casey could've moved that rock if, in fact, it had needed to be moved. The strain of pushing it seemed to exacerbate the pain in her back. But a resigned Melanie knew that's how Margaret was. She wanted to do it herself, no matter the toll.

Not long after that, on September 9th, Melanie got a call from Clara. In an unusually tight voice she said, "I need to talk to you."

Melanie thought something had happened to one of the horses.

But Clara had something more disturbing to tell her. "Margaret was finally hurting so bad yesterday, I ran her down to the emergency room. She's got cancer."

Bracing herself after this news, Melanie said, "Okay. What do you want me to do?"

"I want you to wander over here after a bit. Act like you're showing up like you always do," Clara said. "Don't bring it up. Just come over."

Melanie was glad to do this. She knew that when you get this kind of information, you're not shocked. You're not surprised. But then you are shocked, and you try to absorb what has happened. When it's finally said, you know something's been wrong all along. Margaret had been avoiding this knowledge, but now that it had come, she had to face it. And doing so had to be very, very scary.

Reading the transcript of that talk with Melanie reminded me of a line from poet David Whyte's book about everyday words. On the word "denial" Whyte says, it "is the crossroads between perception and readiness, to deny denial is to invite powers into our lives we have not yet readied ourselves to meet."[2]

Margaret had been denying her pain and what it might mean. But it had reached a point where she could no longer do so. Because she was the person she was, she would somehow ready herself to meet the powers that were now in her life. Powers that were pointing to her death.

Clara faced it with her. Together they investigated possible options.

2 David Whyte. *Consolations: The Solace, Nourishment and Underlying Meaning of Everyday Words*. Langley, WA: Many Rivers Press, 2015, 51.

Margaret took the first round of chemo, but it left her feeling so sick, so nauseated and weak, that she knew she couldn't continue. They contacted Robert Hamilton, a doctor who lived in the area. He arranged for Margaret to be admitted to the University of Texas MD Anderson Cancer Center in Houston, which was in the vanguard of U. S. cancer treatment centers. He even arranged for her to be flown there.

But she was spiraling downward too quickly, and the thought of such travel and staying so far from home overwhelmed her. Their friend Sandy Greene, who had done all that nursing in New Mexico, New York, and then in Colorado, offered to help, and her offer was gratefully accepted. Home health care, then Hospice via Lora Palermo, a long-time neighbor and friend.

September 9th, when Melanie received the call, to October 29th, the day Margaret died, seven weeks, held great trials and heartache for the Singing Acres community. Emergency trips to the Pueblo hospital, friends and home health care pitching in where possible, people coming by for their final visits, a few high points and dramatic lows marked those final weeks.

On that Monday, Hospice had been in, leaving in the early afternoon. Sandy was with Margaret, and Clara and Melanie were administering what Melanie called "Clara's famous hydrotherapy" to Clara's injured horse. Melanie and Scott had found the animal up in the pasture cut by barbed wire the day before. The therapy involved spraying cold water on the injury, which acted as an ice pack, bringing blood to the wound and helping with circulation and healing.

The two were intent on their task when out of the blue, Melanie heard Clara say, "Yup. That's it. I think we'd better get in the house."

As they walked through the doorway, Sandy met them. She was on her way to tell them Margaret was gone.

AFTER THE FUNERAL, AFTER THE MEMORIAL SERVICE AND THE SPREADing of the ashes, life was quieter at the ranch, but work still needed to be done. The animals and the ranch itself needed continued attention. At Clara's request, Melanie became the foreman, taking on more responsibility for all that had to be done.

Almost eight years later, loyal, smart, competent Melanie is still doing her job, and her doing it means Clara can stay on the ranch. Clara says it wouldn't be possible without Melanie, who can and is willing to do anything that needs to be done.

Melanie causes me to think of poet Marge Piercy, who wrote a poem that has become a favorite of mine. The poem begins, "The people I love the best/ jump into work head first … " Later comes a metaphor of strength and steadfastness, "I love people who harness themselves, an ox to a heavy cart … who do what has to be done, again and again."[3]

The poem, "To Be of Use," to me describes the steadfast foreman at Singing Acres Ranch. She once asked the question, "Who ARE those ladies?" And through the years, she came to know, and she became one of them.

---

3 "To Be of Use," *Circles on the Water*. New York: Alfred A. Knopf, 1994, 106.

PART III
Relatively Speaking

Is that you? Circa 2008. Author photo.

15

Word from Down Under

O<small>N THE OTHER SIDE OF THE WORLD IN THE TINY TOWN OF N</small>OOJEE, Victoria, southern Australia, a normal day in early 2006 began with an ordinary tiresome task. An Australian Margaret Locarnini sat at her desk, phone pressed to ear, on hold with her insurance company. Knowing she was in for a long wait as she progressed through the queue, with her computer in front of her, she decided to amuse herself. Searching the Internet for topics that randomly came to mind, she eventually tapped in her own name, wondering what might pop up. She knew her results would be different from her famous brother who worked with the World Health Organization and who had hundreds of entries. She knew because she'd done a search on him before. But not on herself. Now she was curious about what the Internet might have to say about her, if anything.

To her surprise, a result appeared. There her name was, right there on the screen, but it was associated with a newspaper, the *Wet Mountain Tribune* in a place she'd never heard of, Westcliffe, Colorado, in the U.S. And the name appeared in an unlikely notice—cleaning duty at a church. But it was there, her name, Margaret Locarnini, on the roster.

"Oh, my god, there's another Margaret Locarnini out there!" she shouted to the computer. Her mind raced even as she emailed the *Tribune*, an unknown newspaper in a foreign land. "I'm a Margaret Locarnini in Australia, and you seem to have a Margaret Locarnini in Colorado. I would really like to contact her," she wrote.

Before long a reply came. Jim Little, owner and editor of the *Tribune*, wrote to confirm there was a Margaret Locarnini in the area. After that, Margaret thought he must have contacted the Colorado Margaret to tell her there was a crazy person in Australia who wanted to get in touch and thought email might work the best for initial contact.

Within a few days, Australia Margaret, usually called Margie or Marg but soon to be known as "Aussie," received an email message from a Becky Sewell, whom she would come to learn was, with husband Jimmy, neighbor and long-time friend of Margaret's and Clara's. The Sewells were also the only people nearby who had Internet access and email and when asked, they were pleased to help the Margarets communicate. So with Becky as intermediary, messages began to flow between Singing Acres and Noojee.

Intriguing to both Margarets, the email exchanges revealed information through which they began to think it possible they were distant cousins. If that were the case, Marg knew from what Margaret had told her, she would be Margaret's only living relative. She wanted to know more and decided the time had come for a phone conversation. It didn't occur to her that the medium could present a bigger problem than either Margaret anticipated. With Marg initiating the call and Margaret answering, the conversation began something like this:

"Hello?" from Colorado.

"Hello. Is this Margaret?" from Australia.

Then from Colorado, "Are you speaking English?"

Marg wondered the same thing, although she could make out a word sometimes. The little time lag on the phone, added to unfamiliar accents and pronunciations, made conversation difficult. But both being Margaret Locarninis, they persevered, eventually finding a rhythm, a routine in which, if Marg enunciated very slowly and carefully, Margaret could understand her. And vice versa.

They continued with occasional calls, but email proved less stressful, so they relied mostly on it. Through their correspondence they discovered, in Marg's words, "amazing things they held in common." They both "went out into the wilds away from cities, both had done teaching, both lived with a woman housemate, and they both had been 'crafty' and artistic."

They talked of meeting, of Marg coming to Colorado. In Marg's mind, this would have to be a visit down the road, after she'd resolved some difficult issues she was in the middle of. She needed to be at home until then. But as Geoffrey Chaucer wrote some seven centuries ago, "Time and tide wait for no man,"[1] or woman.

In the spring of 2007 an email arrived from Becky, one Margaret hadn't requested. Becky had taken the bold step of telling Marg that Margaret wasn't well. That if she really wanted to see her, she should probably plan a trip sooner rather than later. The communiqué alarmed Marg and prompted action.

With a break coming up from her freelance work auditing nursing homes, she put other pressing issues aside and booked a June flight to Colorado. She would be at Singing Acres for almost two weeks.

She didn't know how it would feel to be on a ranch in the American West. Or to meet Margaret, to have found another Margaret Locarnini only to possibly lose her soon after. But she knew she had to go, otherwise she would always wonder.

She did wonder how it must feel from Margaret's perspective, knowing she may indeed have a living relative. And one in Australia, the other side of the world. They hadn't known each other existed a year and a half ago. Their exchanges by email and phone had led them to think they really did want to see and get to know each other. They both were curious about the other and excited by the prospect of meeting. It would have been natural had there been some misgivings, some worry about it not being what they hoped but, if so, those worries weren't much on their radar screens. Marg was making this trip, and Margaret was glad she was coming.

The meeting of the two Margarets triggered a range of emotions, delight among them. Marg adjusted easily enough to being called Aussie, and both were more than pleased with the opportunity to learn further about their other-side-of-the-world counterpart. But knowing Margaret as I did, I wasn't surprised when, years later, Aussie told me how she'd

1 Geoffrey Chaucer, "The Clerk's Tale," *The Canterbury Tales*, 1395.

been tested by someone expert at it. How Margaret was out to learn whether this Australian was tough enough to claim the Locarnini name she was so proud of.

The first hint of the testing came when Aussie, knowing her manners and wanting to be a considerate guest, offered to help prepare dinner. She was glad when Margaret took her up on it, not knowing she would be put her in charge of a task new to her, cleaning and preparing prairie oysters, also known as Rocky Mountain oysters. Testicles from bulls, and in some places, sheep and pigs, prairie oysters presented a "delicacy" Aussie hadn't encountered before. At least not until Margaret went to the big chest freezer, lifted the lid and pulled out a plastic bag. She handed it to Aussie. "Okay. You can cook these."

Explaining what was in the bag, Margaret crossed her arms, leaned against the cupboard, and waited to see if her guest was really up for it. In true Locarnini fashion, Aussie didn't miss a beat. She nonchalantly removed the seemingly soccer-ball-size objects from the bag, set them in the dish rack and began her work—defrosting, peeling, washing, rolling them in flour and then frying them. She chatted casually with Margaret as she worked.

Supper on the table, she, Margaret and Clara sat down to eat. By the time the meal was over, she knew she'd passed the first test. Not a single oyster was left.

Aussie suspected there would be further tests, and confirmation came the next day. This trial came in a ride around the ranch in Margaret's old Toyota, a car Margaret had already told her would go anywhere. Aussie noted that Margaret meant what she'd said: they went everywhere. She also thought Margaret seemed to choose the roughest tracks and ensure the tires leaned at sharp angles on the steep mountainsides. They went through brush, under trees, up, down, and most certainly all around. Aussie knew what she was up to. She thought, She's trying to see whether I have the balls to be a Locarnini.

After a harrowing, gut-shaking ride, Aussie gathered Margaret had her answer. Turning toward Aussie, she said, "You don't scare easily, do you?"

Aussie breathed quietly, relaxing the last of terror's hold on her insides, not wanting any hint of it to show. Then she looked at Margaret coolly and smiled.

Knowing she wasn't through all the tests and that hunting claimed an important place in Margaret's life, Aussie prepared herself for an encounter with guns. She was aware that Margaret had learned shooting and hunting from her father, making it even more significant. And Margaret had put a whole lot of food on the table for a whole lot of people through hunting. Aussie knew Margaret wondered how was she to deal with this supposed Locarnini who didn't even know how to shoot. The answer to this unspoken question came soon. Aussie would have shooting lessons.

Margaret and Clara's friend Curtis instructed Aussie. She learned to use a handgun, a shotgun, and a rifle, with which she did well. But when Margaret wanted her to take one of each of those weapons back to Australia with her, Aussie begged off, citing Customs as a barrier. She didn't know if Customs would be a problem but in truth, guns weren't her cup of tea.

Neither were the four-wheelers she and Margaret rode, screaming around the ranch and up and down the highway. One afternoon, they left the house around 4:30. By that time of day Margaret had downed a couple of drinks. Aussie suspected the drinks were a way of coping with the very real pain Margaret didn't talk about but must have been experiencing. The way she moved, the lines around her eyes, the manner of her teasing, which could become more challenging than lighthearted. These were telltale signs. She wouldn't have needed those years of work in the health care system to recognize them.

On this afternoon, each on her own four-wheeler, Aussie watched Margaret drive maniacally, defiantly, leaving her far behind. She didn't much want to go at that pace, whether on the dirt or highway. She preferred moderate speeds at best. When she'd seen no sign of her host for a while, she figured Margaret must have gone back to the house. She was surprised when she spotted Margaret coming to find her. Relieved, too, because her four-wheeler had run out of gas.

Sitting at the side of the highway, she vacillated between appreciation and exasperation as Margaret drove up. Margaret's greeting didn't help the vacillation. She grinned and said, "Yeah, I didn't think you'd have enough gas to make it home."

Aussie met these tests as she did everything else—straightforwardly and with determination. She didn't much mind a challenge, vexing as they could be, because she knew she could rise to it. She understood what Margaret was doing, guessing that after being without family, she may have felt nervous about the possibility of Aussie really being related to her. But Margaret apparently got over that hurdle, just as Aussie got over those Margaret had set for her.

When Margaret invited her to go fishing at her special place on the Petersen ranch, Aussie recognized this as the rare privilege it was. She'd heard Margaret didn't take just anyone to that spot. Now they could relax and get to know each other, no barriers, no agendas.

Now their conversation flowed more amiably and open-heartedly. They learned small things and large about each other. They both had Ann as a middle name. Their fathers also had the exact same names, Jack Locarnini. Neither had known their fathers much and had little sense of their fathers' histories. Both believed both sides of their families had originated in a small village in Italy. The story they held in common was that in the 1850s gold rush, half of the boys in the family had gone to California, the other half to Australia. Margaret liked to tell Aussie, "The intellectuals went to California, and the hillbillies went to Australia."

Margaret may have softened, but she was still Margaret. Aussie saw it as another opportunity to smile benignly at her likely cousin. In fact, she loved Margaret's sense of humor and her unwillingness to put up with any hint of deception.

They couldn't prove they were related beyond a general family tree with its roots in Italy, a tree with many deviating branches. But, as Aussie told me, given how they'd both always acutely felt the lack of family, they "were keen to adopt each other, and we did." By the time Aussie went home, they felt very much like family to each other, regardless of technicalities.

Aussie planned a second trip, this one a September birthday surprise for Margaret, whose birthday fell on the 26th. It was her seventieth. But a lot had happened in the few months between the first trip and the second. By the time Aussie arrived, Margaret had gotten the diagnosis of advanced-stage pancreatic cancer, and she was in the hospital. Aussie went there to see her and learned Margaret wasn't happy to see her newfound cousin, despite the pains Aussie had taken to visit.

Aussie tried to explain to her, "But I'd planned to come as a birthday surprise. That's why I'm here."

Margaret countered, "You're here only because you think I'm going to drop off the earth."

"I'm here because I'd already planned it."

This was obviously a Locarnini exchange, and it pointed to Margaret's old fears. She didn't want anyone suggesting in any way that she wasn't going to be around very long.

Discharged from the hospital and back at home, Margaret wanted to cook a meal for some friends and her Australian relation. Naturally there were protests, and naturally they were ignored. Aussie told me she would never forget the image of Margaret as she barbequed giant steaks for everyone with one hand and held up her pants with the other. She'd lost so much weight even her belts wouldn't do the job.

But the visit, despite Margaret's rapidly declining health and another rocky beginning, turned out to be another exceptional one. Questions that had arisen between visits, some springing from what they'd learned from each other in June, took them into many deep conversations. Their topics ranged from family to the straw bale house Aussie and her partner, also a Margaret and called Marg, were building. Already underway, it was to be an ecologically sound, practical and beautiful home.

Aussie told Margaret and Clara that her mum had contributed two straw bales for the house. Loving the idea of contributing, they wanted to do so themselves, but they had more in mind. They wanted to contribute a whole wall. Aussie protested that this was too much, but Margaret and Clara had their way in the end. Aussie decreed the wall would be dedicated to Singing Acres Ranch.

They had a choice of which wall it was to be. On the east would be the Croissant & Coffee wall, or they could put dibs on the Gin & Tonic wall, on the west. Margaret and Clara chose the east, the side from which you can watch the sun come up. Now it's finished, complete with the Singing Acres Ranch logo, a mosaic fashioned from broken pottery, the making of which Margaret would have loved, including four horseshoes she contributed. The sun rises on that logo every day, on both sides of the world.

Margaret died just a few weeks after Aussie returned to Australia. Aussie's third trip that year came in December for her newfound cousin's memorial service, held on a favorite rock outcropping behind the ranch house. When she went home to Noojee that time, she carried some of Margaret's ashes with her.

Through these visits, Aussie and Clara became close friends, and in the Singing Acres manner, extended family. That family brought many Westcliffe friendships to Aussie, friendships that are nurtured through various forms of correspondence.

In 2009, Aussie traveled again to Westcliffe, this time partner Marg Bailey with her. They wanted to celebrate Clara's seventy-second birthday with Clara—in person. Aussie visited again in 2011, knowing she might not be able to return, that life's demands at home would likely keep her there. And knowing that as much as Clara dislikes airplanes and travel in general, she's not likely to go there.

But these days on an ordinary Sunday, every Sunday, a phone call comes to Clara. It's from a Margaret Locarnini in tiny town called Noojee on the other side of the world.

16

Hardy Stock

"**H**EY. YOU NEED MORE STORIES?" BENNY HOLLERED, HIS BIG, CHEERY voice booming from his large frame, his face overtaken by a wide, mischievous grin.

I'd walked down from the ranch house's stone steps to the yard, just as he'd pulled up in his black SUV, with his delightful, spunky wife Bridgette, and two friends Beth and Eric Eslinger, visiting from Kansas. He knew I was there to talk more with his Aunt Clara Mary about the book. He, Bridgette, and friends were there to wish Clara a happy birthday.

"I'm here to see if I've gotten the stories right that I already have," I answered.

"Well, I may not be right," Benny shot back, "but I am colorful."

Those words, I thought, defined his very essence. Benny is colorful. A big guy with a big personality, he's Clara's nephew, son of Gale, Clara's late older brother. Just in the last year, he and Bridgette had sold their place in Rago, and were happily ensconced in the house that Mike Haga and David Brothers had built back in the mid-1990s. And that meant they lived close to Clara, which suited everybody.

I'd met Benny a number of times over the years. The first time, in the late 1990s, he came to the ranch house when I was visiting Margaret and Clara. All Clara had said was, "This is Carol."

Next thing I knew, I was swept up in muscular arms, being swung around and around, like a little kid. A big laugh erupted from deep inside him, along with the words, "Well, howdy, Carol!"

Benny and some motorcycling friends had been to Cripple Creek, a picturesque old mining town nearby, now a gambling haven, having a grand time. I thought they must have a grand time pretty often. They'd stopped by on their way back to Kansas.

Benny, with his leather vest, tattooed arms, long hair and beard was nothing but colorful then, although I was too astonished to think of the word at the time. On subsequent encounters, I'd prepare myself for a hearty greeting from Benny, and I was never disappointed.

In the spring of 2012, David and I set out for Abbyville, Kansas to attend his cousin Glenna Dellenbach's ninetieth birthday celebration. Abbyville lies about an hour's drive from Rago, where Clara's old home place is. Her younger brother, Ray, lives there, and at that time, Benny still lived on adjacent land. We decided we couldn't pass up the opportunity to see him again and to meet Ray.

We'd phoned ahead, so both Benny and Ray were expecting us. Following Benny's directions that came complete with landmarks—this wheat field, that oil pump, the old schoolhouse—we found his house. Sitting on a bit of a hill, it looked out on trees, meadows, and fields.

A handwritten sign on the door greeted us. "Open the door and holler! Promise I won't shoot." We followed the instructions, and Benny, as promised, didn't shoot. He did, however, treat us to a delightful hour or so of stories, some in response to our questions, others that flowed naturally from our conversation, starting with the house itself.

It had been there when Rudolph, his great-grandfather, bought the land near the end of the 1880s. Over the years, with several additions, it grew to about three times the original size, not unlike the ranch house at Singing Acres. At the time, Benny was making more improvements, redoing the kitchen.

We sat in the living room across from a striking rock fireplace. Benny told us the rock came from Singing Acres Ranch. Quartz from one of the old mines back up on the north side of the property, just like the fireplace at Singing Acres. The cedar framing it came from a tree that once sat where we were sitting, before the room had been added. Benny's great-grandpa, Rudolph, had planted it, and Benny had wanted to keep the wood when he had to cut it down to build the room.

The way Benny talked about the place brought to mind poet David Whyte's ruminations that "memory is a pulse passing through all created life ... all the while creating a continual but almost untouchable *now*."[1] The very essence of the room, of the house was built on memories. And here was the cedar as continual, touchable evidence.

Benny told us about his dad, Gale, about how, when Gale was a tot, he'd gotten thrown in the river wearing the full cotton gown babies were dressed in early in the 1920s. It happened when the river bridge blocked an overflow of water forcing it around so it washed out a big hole. When the river when down, the hole trapped a bunch of fish. Everybody in the community went to the hole and were "catching the hell out of catfish," according to Benny.

His grandma was fishing, too, with baby Gale perched on her lap. She got a strong bite, with the cork bobbing maniacally. In her excitement, she jumped to her feet, propelling baby Gale into the river. "He sank like a rock," Benny told us, "and Aunt Valentine jumped in after him. He survived that one!"

As an overview of further misadventures, Benny gave us this rundown. "When he got a little older, he drank some dirty water down on the river and got typhoid fever. He damn near died from that. Then later he jumped out of a hay mound and landed on a pitch fork and cut his jugular vein. Grandpa had to haul him into town and get that fixed. He survived that one, too, of course. But then he got clotheslined two or three times with the horse."

That wasn't all. Benny continued, "I don't remember what happened by the time he went in the military, but he was in all of the big ones: Africa, Sicily, Italy and Belgium and all of those countries, England, France, Czechoslovakia and Germany. Battle of the Bulge and all. Survived that. Had malaria eight times, three or four overseas and then back here, attacks after he got home. He drew disability, around ten dollars a month, for a couple of years, till they finally quit sending it."

Whew, I thought. No wonder Benny was so tough. Gale for a father

---

1 Ibid,143.

and Clara for an aunt. Clara once told me she'd suffered four serious concussions, two from being bucked off horses, one when she fell off a high load of hay, and one in a car accident. No permanent damage from any of them. Hardy stock, those Reidas.

I asked, "You were in Viet Nam, weren't you? In the Army?"

"Army. First Cav," Benny explained. "Yup. I got lucky. I didn't get shot, but they got close several times."

He went on, "I'm one hundred per cent disabled because of PTSD. I went through a ninety-day program at the Topeka Hospital and learned a lot, why I was the way I was. I'm a card-carrying son-of-a-bitch."

Although I wasn't sure I agreed with that assessment, I could tell Benny enjoyed giving it. More color.

As for his Aunt Clara Mary, he told us she was "a helluva good teacher. She got respect from all her students, every one of them."

He admired his aunt's strength in many ways, but the physical aspect really made an impression. "When she was still here on the farm, she was milking cows, and she had this muscle here," he said, pointing to his bicep, "that would stand up about that high and that wide. Her hands ain't very big, but when she got a hold of you, she'd put you on your knees."

Benny told us about Clara's first teaching job up on the north side of Wichita, where she took knives away from kids and made them toe the line. "They thought she was a pushover, but she was tougher than hell."

When David commented, "Put those two together, Margaret and Clara, you've got two tough people," Benny laughed.

"I could handle Margaret alright. I wasn't scared of her, though she thought I was," he said.

He talked about their trips to Cripple Creek to gamble. He'd win a little and Margaret would try to get him give her the money so he wouldn't lose it. They'd argue about it, and someone would always be listening. Noticing that, Benny would say to them, "This is the meanest goddamn woman I've ever known. Look at her taking my money."

Benny looked lost in thought for a moment, then said, "I had good times with her. I guess she went out like she wanted to."

He talked about how Margaret was offered the chance to go to the M.D. Anderson Center in Texas, but decided not to, saying, "No, I wanna' die here. I don't wanna die in Texas."

In a reflective mood, Benny told us about how his dad told stories and how he wished he'd had a video camera to record them. Or how he wished he'd paid more attention to the stories at the time. He did remember his dad talking about Great-Grandpa Rudolph and his belief that for every language you can speak you live another life. Rudolph could speak German, French, Czech and English, and he taught his children Czech. But Arnold would never teach his children to speak the language. Benny thought that strange.

"You know there are quite a number of stories like that from that age because immigrants, and especially children of immigrants, wanted their kids growing up American," David offered, "not holding on to the old country."

"That makes me think about the argument from way back about the spelling of our name," Benny said. "There's 'RAIDA and there's REIDA. Rudolph and a brother got here, and one decided they wanted to change the spelling to look more American, but keep the pronunciation. One decides on RAIDA, and another on the other spelling. We all still argue about it. Supposedly from the old country it's spelled REJDA, or the RA's say RAJDA, so what are you going to do?"

According to Benny there are Reidas in Nebraska who still spell the name REJDA. Through some previous research, I'd learned it wasn't unusual before and in the early part of the twentieth century to have different spellings of a name. Some of the differences came from the way census takers, tax collectors, county clerks, and other officials spelled it. Occasionally it came from the way officials at Ellis Island recorded one. But the desire to Americanize names was strong, adhering to the melting pot idea, so there was plenty of freedom to change the spelling as one thought fit. And, as it seems the Reida/Raida family did.

This topic came up again when David and I visited Ray. Leaving

Benny, we headed straight over to Ray's house, continuing on smooth dirt roads, through green fields, and by the occasional oil pump. Ray lived on the old home place, and while the old house has been replaced by a new home, I recognized a number of landmarks from Clara's stories.

We didn't drive through the creek as countless Reidas had done for decades, as Margaret had done on her first visit and many times after. We drove over it on a bridge Ray had built. I could see, however, what it must have meant to take a car through the stream, particularly up and down its banks and during high-water times. Challenging many times, impossible others.

As we came to the house, in the yard close by I saw the old windmill standing tall, the windmill that had powered so much over the years. It reminded me of how Arnold, Clara's father, had charged batteries for the radio on a little windmill perched atop the tractor shed some seven decades ago. It stood near where the old barn had been, where Clara's mother, Mae, must have been walking when she saw her son Gale returning from the war. When she whirled those pails of milk, overcome by surprise and the excitement of seeing him after four long years. Imagining the scene brought a lump to my throat.

An intense green surrounded us—thick, sprawling lawn, new crops in the fields, and towering trees that bordered the creek and beyond, undoubted havens on hot summer days.

Ray came out to greet us as we parked the car, apologizing that his wife, Joyce, couldn't be there to meet us. She and their daughter, Sandra, had gone to Wichita for the day. I was taken by Ray's strong resemblance to Clara, both in looks and manner. Warm, genuine, and welcoming, he showed us around, answering our questions and pointing out things that might interest us.

He told us about Hopewell School that lay a mile or two away. "It was a one-room school house," Ray said. "We rode horses most of the time, Clara and me. There were twenty-some kids and only four that weren't Reidas."

I remembered that Clara was five years older than Ray, something he soon confirmed. "Everyone in our family graduated from that little country school except me. When Clara graduated from eighth grade and went on to Adams School, I went there with her, to third grade."

We walked over to a small building, fondly called Arnold's Lodge, which had replaced the old granary Arnold had used for myriad purposes. Now it seemed a quiet refuge with comfortable chairs, intriguing pictures and other memorabilia lining the walls, and a beautiful saddle, one that had been well used and well cared for, placed on a table in front of an old, restored wagon wheel.

Ray bought the saddle in Kingman many years ago for about thirty-five dollars. He'd ridden on it for a while but then no longer needed it, so he gave it to Clara back in the late 1960s. She'd used it in their riding program and otherwise. Years later, Clara had the saddle refurbished and asked Ray if he'd like to have it back. He said yes, and there the saddle, with all its history, sat.

We moved back toward the house, the overcast sky and sprinkles of rain powerless to dampen our lively conversation, despite the tornado warning we'd all heard earlier. We saw distant lightning, accompanied by rolls of thunder, but the weather served only to bring us more of this Reida's story.

On summer vacation from high school, Ray had been working on a tractor, spring toothing, which I learned was a second step in preparing the soil for planting. A spring tooth is attached to and pulled along by the tractor, smoothing the soil for planting. The man he worked for, Paul Simons, was on another tractor. What looked like a "little bitty cloud" came up, but Ray wasn't concerned about it. Paul had a different reaction, waving Ray over to tell him, "We better unhook and go to the house. I saw lightning in that cloud and I don't like the looks of it."

They started for the house on their Minneapolis Molines, tractors that would run pretty fast in road gear. Ray remembered them heading across the field, and that was it. The next thing he knew —five days later—he awoke in a hospital. Lightning had hit him square in the chest, leaving a wide, deep burn across it. It had knocked him off the tractor, which then went into a ditch, and then rolled over. The bang from the lightning also stunned Paul, who had been near Ray, but Paul had hand clutches and was able to stop his machine.

A man across the road who'd had a problem with his pickup saw it happen. Thankfully, he got the pickup started and they loaded Ray into the back and took him to the house, thinking he was dead. But just in case he wasn't, Ray was then transferred to the car and, because the doctor wasn't in at Harper Hospital, was taken to Anthony Hospital. There he spent several days being cared for before being taken back to Harper, where he finally woke up.

It took a long time for Ray to recover from the lightning strike. For years, he was tired, every bone in his body ached, and he went from one hundred ninety-five pounds to one hundred forty. He was unable to play sports, and when finally he did play some, it took all he had. After years of persistence, of determination, he regained much of what he'd lost, although he's lived all his life with chronic pain. But he comes from hardy Reida stock and he gets on with things.

Ray was keen on showing us his grandfather's naturalization certificate, and we were equally eager to see it. Sure enough, there with the official seal of the United States of America, on the 11th day of June, 1892, Rudolph Reida, a native of Austria, was declared A CITIZEN OF THE UNITED STATES.

Curious about why Austria was listed as his county, I later learned that at the time, Moravia, Czechoslovakia, where Rudolph was born, was under Austrian rule. But the people were Czech, also known as Bohemian. I wrote earlier that Rudolph had not wanted to go into the Austrian army to fight for the emperor. That's why he came to this country.

A book that later came my way, *The [Czech]²s (Bohemians) in America*, written by Thomas Capek in 1919, tells of how the great Czech immigration really gained speed in the mid-nineteenth century, partly due to political persecution of those who supported the revolution of 1848.

---

2 Brackets indicate a common spelling of Czech. The title of the book uses Cech, but using a symbol not included on many computers.

In the process of researching her Bohemian mother's ancestry, my friend and neighbor Harriet Simons came across this book, which she lent to me. I opened it randomly and there lay words that seemed to describe Rudolph himself. "Idealism is the most precious offering of the [Czech] immigrant to America. Without ideals even practical America is unthinkable."[3]

Rudolph had come to this country with ideals, and those principles of honesty, trustworthiness, commitment to community, family and friends were still very much evident in the Reidas I'd come to know.

After showing us the certificate, several vintage photographs of Rudolph, his wife Mary, and others, Ray had another treat for us. A compilation of the Reida genealogy. It was then that the conversation returned to spelling. The book lists these: Reda, Rada, Rejda, Reida, Raida.

The book traces the family back to Frank and Antonia, who were Clara's great-grandparents. It goes back further, but because it was difficult to trace and verify records when the book was begun some sixty years ago, it's possible some of the earlier research would come out differently now.

Yet it helped me to navigate my way through some of the family history, keeping me straight on five generations of Reidas. I found it fascinating, perhaps because I can trace my family back only to my maternal grandparents, who died before my parents even met, as did my paternal grandparents. My father left the rest of his family behind when he left New York for good. Family I never knew. Margaret must have felt this fascination, too. Perhaps she knew more about hers since she did have a chance to know her grandparents a little, but in the end, she had only Aussie, a gift, indeed.

Ray offered to let me take the book, a generous and kind gesture. It helped ground me many times as I made my way through the stories, the lives of the Reidas. His genial hospitality illustrated why Clara's one regret was not living closer to him, not getting to spend more time with him.

---

3 Classic Reprint Series, Forgotten Books, 2012, p. x(*www.forgottenbooks.org*) First publication by Houghton Mifflin Company, Boston and New York, 1920.

Just as with Benny, I'd met Clara's next oldest sister, Virginia, at the ranch although in a less startling fashion. She came to stay a couple of times for extended periods after Margaret died and when Clara had hip replacement surgery. Five years older than Clara, she claimed to be a 1932 model while Clara was a 1937. Her lively sense of humor complemented Clara's, and between the two of them, it seemed there were few dull moments and lots of mischief.

Their late sister Zelda, who was eighteen years older than Clara, married and had a family when Clara was still a child and Virginia not yet a teenager. Zelda lived in other states for many years, and opportunities for the siblings to be together were few. But letters and phone calls kept them in touch, and they enjoyed the occasions they could spend time with each other. And now Clara and Virginia were really making the most of their time together.

David and I didn't get to see Virginia on the trip to Kansas, but I did get to talk with her by phone beforehand. We'd had some good exchanges in 2011 when she'd had one of those longer stays at Singing Acres. In 2011 her visit had overlapped with Aussie Margaret's trip, and it was before I'd begun writing this book. But our phone conversation was most helpful. With that feet-on-the-ground Reida warmth, she helped me get a clearer picture of their early family life.

When Virginia was born, she almost starved to death because her mother didn't have enough milk, and infant Virginia wouldn't easily take a bottle. Because of this, she was a spindly little one, and Arnold and Mae almost lost her. Through this shaky beginning, Arnold catered to her with the result, as Virginia said, she "became a daddy's girl."

At that time, babies slept with their parents, and Virginia got five years of that until Clara came along. Then they had to move Virginia out of their bed, so Clara could be there. But rather than having Virginia sleep with Zelda, which would have been the common practice, her father put a cot right by his bed and he'd hold her hand until she went to sleep.

Virginia remembered how much her dad loved the farm and that his brothers lived nearby. The brothers enjoyed going into town to play dominoes and visit with people, but Arnold liked staying at the farm. When her mother, Mae, would take little Clara with her to sell eggs and buy groceries in town, Virginia and her dad would go out in the fields and find pretty rocks and pick daisies.

As she grew older and the U. S. entered World War II, she watched as her brother and cousins were drafted. She was the oldest one left at home, so she became a field hand, with her dad riding the tractor and her doing whatever needed to be done. Virginia always suspected that Clara envied her getting to work with their dad, rather than going to town or doing housework, and that was confirmed when, in a recent visit Clara told her, "I had to stay in the house. You got to go to the field."

And in sisterly fashion, Virginia said, "Well, that's just too bad."

After Clara moved to Colorado, Virginia drove their mother out to see her several times. Falling in love with the mountains, she found the ranch charming, although she immediately recognized its challenges. Clara had told her how everyone who came out to see her and Margaret was enchanted by the place, usually saying how they'd like to live there. But, Virginia suspected they had no idea what it took to do that.

"When they first landed there," Virginia said, "I know the natives didn't think they'd last more than six months. But they didn't know what they were dealing with."

She related some of the story of their grandfather and how he'd come to this country and worked hard enough as a carpenter and a farmer to raise a family and provide at least one hundred twenty acres for each of the seven children. And how her father had done something similar. He and her mother had both been such strong, good people.

Far from the sentiment evoked by Mark Twain, who said, "I do not like work even when someone else does it,"[4] the Reidas all seemed to see the value of hard work, regardless of who was doing it. From Rudolph and Mary to Arnold and Mae, and the children they raised, they all met challenges and they all prevailed.

---

4 Jon Winokur. *The Portable Curmudgeon.* New York: Signet/Penguin, 1987, 289.

Clara knew that working hard was important and she didn't mind it a bit. But she also knew education was essential. She told me about seeing her mother, who had no schooling beyond eighth grade, struggle after Clara's father died so young and how that impressed the importance of education upon her.

Its importance was underlined when Clara graduated from high school and her brother Gale asked her, "What are you going to do with your life?"

"Either go on to college or join the armed services," she answered.

"If you go to college, I'll do all I can to help you. If you join the service, you're no sister of mine," Gale said, reminded of his experiences in war. Clara made her decision right on the spot.

Graduating from college, becoming a teacher not only fulfilled her desire to work with and help young people, it helped support her through the lean years of ranching. Teaching, riding camps, the ski area, the tree business and breeding horses all made their demands on her, and not only did she never begrudge a bit of it, she seemed to thrive on it all.

Returning to Thoreau, who had such an impact on Clara's students that they encouraged her onward, I saw something from his *Journal* that seemed to speak to what these robust and resilient people knew well. Observing his neighbor, a farmer who seemed to embody the poetry of farming, Thoreau wrote "He does nothing with haste and drudgery, but as if he loved it. He makes the most of his labor, and takes infinite satisfaction in every part of it."[5]

To me, this further describes the Reidas I know and know of. Full of stories, they enjoy life; they're hardy, colorful, and satisfied in their labor.

---

5 *The Journal of Henry David Thoreau*, 1837-1861. New York: New York Review of Books Classics, 2009, from Fall 1851.

Part IV
The View from Singing Acres

Meadows and mountains of Singing Acres. Sangre de Cristo range in the background, 2015. Author photo.

17

"THE WILDFLOWERS ARE SPECTACULAR THIS YEAR," CLARA SAID. "YOU wouldn't believe how tall the Indian paintbrush are. We can go see them if you want to."

"I want to!" I all but shouted.

We climbed into Clara's pickup and she drove along the north side of the ranch on the dirt road that goes by the SAR corral across from Sandy's place and Clara's guesthouse. We passed Bridgette's and Benny's then dropped down a bit by Melanie's house, which sat in a long, gorgeous valley. Prolific, wildflowers dotted the pastures and meadows on both sides of us, and a few of the Sangre de Cristo Mountains gleamed with their last streaks of snow between the smaller, verdant Wet Mountains.

It had been an exceptional year for Colorado with precipitation far above the annual average of thirteen inches for the Wet Mountain Valley, and now the valley was showing off. Given those snow-dotted peaks and the thick greenness everywhere, the wildflowers weren't the only spectacular sight. Added in, the scene was stunning.

"Sandy's mother used to love to watch us round up and drive horses down this valley when we leased some of these pastures for our herd. Sandy would do gate duty, and Helen watched from the truck," Clara told me.

I could easily picture Clara and Margaret, exuberant and dexterous, working hard and having the time of their lives, on their horses loping down that valley toward an excited and appreciative Helen and Sandy. The scene was so vivid in my mind, it almost made me cry.

We then drove back and up into the forest along a barely legible track. I was in charge of opening gates, a much easier task than driving over the deep gullies heavy rain had washed in the erstwhile road. The story of Aussie and the ride Margaret had taken her on came to mind, and I thanked my lucky stars Clara was at the wheel.

After we wove around trees, passed through a couple of gates and over several tricky spots on the trail, Clara brought the truck to a halt on a high bluff. She explained that we were on the top of the mountain right behind the ranch house, but because of the quarter-mile of trees and mounded terrain below, we couldn't see it.

I'd never been to this part of the ranch. I'd always been awed by the beauty of places I had been, those meadows and forests I tried to describe earlier, but this was beauty squared. On this day and in that place, everything seemed "more so." Brilliant red, purple, yellow, and gold wildflowers grew in great profusion. I looked out across the landscape and saw the south meadows of the ranch, the deep green of the ponderosa, spruce, fir and aspen forest marching over the smaller hills in the foreground, and the purple Sangres with their snow fronds reigning in the distance. A sapphire blue sky and puffball clouds floating above the peaks accentuated their grandeur.

The view from Singing Acres and of Singing Acres. All the stories I'd heard seem to come alive again in this setting, a great many that haven't made it into this book. And for each story, I could sense another hundred I didn't know, just as Tanner Camper had suggested when we'd talked earlier that morning. I understood better than ever before that when life is so rich and full, it's not possible to capture it all in a single book. Maybe not even in a series of books.

I felt a sense of Margaret and Clara, when first on this land, learning its ways, taking in its beauty and its challenges, and appreciating those who helped them know how to live and thrive on it. People like Flo and Richard Hardin, who had a sawmill and were always giving them slabs of lumber to build little shelters for their animals. The Hardins sold them their first cow and let them make payments of five dollars a month on her. Margaret and Clara knew they could always count on the Hardin's sons, Jack and Frank, for anything that needed to be done. The whole family was constantly helping them, giving them advice, and it was help and advice they needed and wanted.

When they first got to the ranch, they had that freezer full of meat but no electricity yet at Singing Acres. Neighbors Jess and Alice Kennon told them to bring the pickup to their place and plug it in. That was a lifesaver.

Alice went with them all over the place to help them get a sense of their environs. She taught Margaret about mushrooms—which ones were safe to eat, which to avoid. The Kennons also tutored them about firewood there, how much they'd need, where to get it. They'd go together and get wood for all of them.

Harold Boehm, a close neighbor who did a lot of horseback riding with them, also helped them learn much about their immediate surroundings. One thing he taught them was not to set a piece of pine for a fence post because the ants will eat it up. You have to use cured-out aspen.

Harold let Clara ride his little black mare, telling her she needed to put her spurs on for that horse. Clara showed up to ride and he reiterated that she needed to put her spurs on. She said, "But I have them on," then looked down to see that she did have them on, but upside down. She'd never used spurs before.

Clara was particularly drawn to George Haputa, an old Bohemian who reminded her of her grandfather. He'd let them take their milk cow over to have her bred, and that was a big help. One time when the two of them were there, George asked them to stay for a drink. He served some of his white lightning, and it was so light and smooth, it went down like water. Clara always thought it was a good thing they went on horseback because otherwise they'd never have made it back home.

Then there were Virginia and Darrell Kness, who owned adjoining property and from whom they learned many ins-and-outs of life in the Wet Mountains. The Knesses had four daughters whom Margaret and Clara watched grow up. The youngest worked for them in the riding program.

And Elmer. Elmer Knight and his family would also be life-long friends. His now late wife, Billie, worked for Clara and Margaret, cleaning their house so the ranchers-teachers-ski area owners could tend to other matters. Elmer had a very gentle hand with horses, and Margaret and Clara loved to watch him work with them. One mare that even Clara had trouble catching was like putty in Elmer's hands.

So many stories, so many good people, so many good deeds, good deeds that Clara and Margaret returned and were grateful to be able to. One was to put their land, all of it, into a conservation easement, which meant it could never be developed. After being hounded by property developers wanting to divide the land into thirty-five acre ranchettes, they were at last able to relax knowing the land was safe. The San Isabel Land Protection Trust announced the transaction in its newsletter, describing the ranch this way:

> The Singing Acres Ranch is a scenic jewel that is admired by all who pass along the highway. In addition to scenic and agricultural values, the property serves as important wildlife habitat with a combination of live water, mature mixed conifer forests and open park-like meadows. The San Isabel Land Protection Trust is grateful to Clara and Margaret for serving as model stewards of the land and for protecting the property for future generations to enjoy.[1]

I REMEMBERED HOW HAPPY MARGARET AND CLARA WERE WHEN THEY talked with Brian Riley, then executive director of Land Protection Trust, about doing this. And that brought to mind how our friend the late Paul Snyder took care of the legal work to make it happen, just as he'd done for David and me with Stillpoint, and so many others. Because of that, in true Singing Acres fashion, Paul and wife Marty Frick became part of the ranch's community.

Marty, who was then director of the West Custer Library, interviewed Clara for the library's heritage project, and that recording is in the library for patrons to enjoy. It was a useful resource in writing this book.

I stood looking at the vastness before me. The Colorado landscape

---

1 San Isabel Land Protection Trust Newsletter, Fall, 2006, 4.

had all kinds of room for dreams and for those dreams that had become reality. Clara and Margaret wanted a ranch in the Colorado Rockies. They had an extraordinary one. They dreamed of raising horses. They raised hundreds of them, beautiful Appaloosas. They wanted to nurture friendships, cultivate community, be helpful when and where they could, be kind to others. They wanted to heed Emerson's advice on common sense, Thoreau's on simplifying life, and both writers' counsel to follow one's dream. They wanted to do all of this. And they did.

ACKNOWLEDGEMENTS

The View from My Desk

Looking out on Singing Acres and the Wet Mountains landscape evokes in me a profound sense of what went into shaping Margaret's and Clara's lives there. And now sitting at my desk with the completed manuscript at my side, I am aware of the considerable contributions of so many in the shaping of this book.

First and foremost among them is Clara, who allowed me the long reins to do as I pleased when I'm sure she'd rather have had me on a lunge line, if not in someone else's corral altogether. She endured multiple in-person interviews, countless questions by phone and mail, and all in good humor. She rounded up contacts, phone numbers, documents, photos and also vouched for my credibility when I wanted to interview someone who didn't know me, and in a few cases, some who did. She was patient when I went in directions she didn't expect, poked around in long-untapped memories and tried out different approaches to writing about her life and Margaret's. Her kindness to me during all of this has only increased my respect and love for her.

Others who assisted in the information roundup include Lois Kellenbenz and Jaye Zola, who put their interviewing skills to work when I greatly needed their help. They also aided in other research, as did Laurette Reiff, Charles H. Kerrigan, and Harriet Simons. Jane English deciphered Margaret's many Girl Scout badges, for which I am grateful. Marty Frick and her now late husband, Paul Snyder, invited us to participate in a library-related interview with Clara, which was as much fun as it was enlightening. I wish Paul were here to read the book and tell me if I came close to capturing Clara's "Clara-ness," as he called it. It was a daunting task he set for me, and I can only hope I succeeded in some measure.

My gratitude goes to the many folks who agreed to ride along by graciously submitting to interviews. A list of their names appears forthwith. My appreciation and thanks certainly extend to the numerous friends who were willing and interested in exploring the idea of friendship, what it is, what makes it last, what happens when it falters. I won't attempt to name everyone, but you know who you are. Those conversations enriched my understanding of friendship, just as my friends enrich my life. I can't imagine being without them.

Many thanks to my brother, Bruce Wilson, and sister-in-law, Marty Wilson, for reading early drafts and providing encouragement as well as insight into things I didn't know. Sighting in a gun, for one, information I hope never to use personally but found helpful here.

My gratitude to the Mechau family and the Colorado Springs Fine Arts Center for allowing me to use Frank Mechau's exquisite "5 Horses" drawing. A delightful and fitting coincidence is that he created it in 1937, the year both Margaret and Clara were born.

I am indebted to Jules Marie for expert and speedy transcription. Many thanks to Jules and to Laurette Reiff, two keen sets of eyes, for reading and commenting on the manuscript. This must have felt a bit like checking hooves at the end of a ride. And to Sue Campbell for her book-design wizardry. I appreciate that she's willing to harness her creativity to make this an aesthetically pleasing book.

Spurring me on through it all was Laura Goodman, editor extraordinaire always. I value her wisdom, patient guidance, and faith in my ability to continue learning and writing from my heart. She was masterful in helping me find my way and keeping me on the trail, when sometimes I wanted to run for the barn.

David Chrislip, my wonderful mate, has been beside me all along. He has read more drafts than anyone can imagine, and his suggestions have enhanced this work. We share a love for reading and writing, and his breadth and depth in these areas lead me to broader and deeper thinking. I'm happy to say that he is, in the words of Dale Evans and Roy Rogers, our favorite singing cowpokes, "my final frontier."

I am grateful to you all for your contributions. Where I've strayed or fallen off my mount on this ride, I accept full responsibility, knowing how hard you've all tried to keep me in the saddle.

That's how it looks from where I sit now. Thank you, everyone.

CAROL ANN WILSON
Boulder, Colorado
July 22, 2015

INTERVIEWS

With gratitude to you all for helping bring this book to life

Clara Reida

Sue Bishop

David Brothers

Sherry Campbell

Danny Cartmill

Bette Casapulla ("B")

Michelle & Kevin Chapman

Kris Corey

Melanie Camper Fall

Sandra Greene

Linda Gulinson

Mike Haga

Mildred Halle

Brenda Jackson

Margaret Locarnini (Aussie)

Barbara Macgregor

Virginia Moraga

Arnold Ray Reida

Ben Reida

Helen Royal

Pat & Tom Schulze

Virginia Van Dolah

A personal note from Clara to all the veterinarians and trainers who worked with SAR horses over the years: Thank you for applying your skill, insight, and support to our horses. Without you Margaret and I never would have succeeded.

Bibliography

Appaloosa Journal. June, 1999, Vol. 53, No.5.

Bateson, Mary Catherine. *Full Circles, Overlapping Lives.* New York: Random House, 2000.

Case No. 88CV33, Custer County District Court; TRIAL DISCLOSURE CERTIFICATE OF PLAINTIFF, Jan. 19, 1988.

Chamberlin, J. Edward. *Horse: How the Horse Has Shaped Civilizations.* New York: BlueBridge Books, 2006, 47.

Colorado Springs Sun. "Independent Rancher Enjoys Rugged Life." December 2, 1979, Section E, 1-2.

Dorris, Michael. *A Yellow Raft in Blue Water.* New York: Picador Publishing, 1987.

Ellington, Lucien and Frucht ,Richard, eds. *Eastern Europe: Introduction to the People, Land and Culture.* Santa Barbara, CA: ABC-CLIO, Inc.: 2005.

Emerson, Ralph Waldo. "Circles," *The Works of Ralph Waldo Emerson.* New York: Tudor Publishing Company, 1930.

Fremont County Sun/Trader Food Section "Conversations in the Kitchen: Marge Locarnini/Teacher, hunter, 'fiercely independent." October 3, 1979.

Frost, Robert. "Nothing Gold Can Stay," *Selected Poems of Robert Frost.* New York: Rinehart Editions, 1963.

Haga, Michael. *On the Brink: How to Survive the Coming Great Depression 1993-2000.* Kansas City, MO: Acclaim Publishing Co., 1992.

Pompia, Jon. "Underworld figure dies in Denver." *The Pueblo Chieftain*, July 30, 2014.

Rocky Mountain News. "Teacher, rancher Locarnini touched many lives." Denver, CO, Nov. 6, 2007, Obituaries.

The Harper Herald. Harper, Kansas: Harper High School. Monday, May 20, 1963,Vol. XXVIII, No. 9.

Thoreau, Henry D. *Walden, The Works of Henry D. Thoreau.* New York: Thomas Y. Crowell Co., 1940.

Welty, Eudora and Sharp, Ronald A., eds. *The Norton Book of Friendship.* New York: W.W. Norton & Co.,1991.

Whyte, David. *Consolations: The Solace, Nourishment and Underlying Meaning of Everyday Words*. Langley, WA: Many Rivers Press, 2015, 51.

Websites

ansi.okstate.edu/breeds/horses/appaloosa/

appaloosa.com/association/history.htm

http://appaloosamuseum.org/

brainyquote.com/quotes/keywords/regret.html

bryanchristiansen01.wix.com/bc1960

Eric Jackson, (*www.forbes.com/sites/ericjackson*), 10/18/2012

http://pubs.usgs.gov/wsp/1850b/report.pdf

http://vads.vetmed.vt.edu/demos/Education/display.cfm?ShowMyFile=Organisms/ClPerfFS.htm

Clara, Regal Sophie Tucker, and Carol.

CAROL ANN WILSON, AUTHOR OF AWARD-WINNING *Still Point of the Turning World: The Life of Gia-fu Feng*, lives in Boulder, Colorado. For more information, please visit *www.carolannwilson.info.*

Made in the USA
Columbia, SC
16 November 2022